TALKING TO ARCHITECTS

By the same author

Anarchy in Action
Streetwork: The Exploding School (with Anthony Fyson)
Vandalism
Tenants Take Over
Housing: An Anarchist Approach
The Child in the City
Art and the Built Environment (with Eileen Adams)
Arcadia for All (with Dennis Hardy)
When We Build Again
Goodnight Campers (with Dennis Hardy)
Chartres: The Making of a Miracle
The Allotment: Its Landscape and Culture (with David Crouch)
The Child in the Country
Undermining the Central Line (with Ruth Rendell)
Welcome, Thinner City: Urban Survival in the 1990s
Images of Childhood (with Tim Ward)
Talking Houses
Talking Schools
Freedom To Go: After the Motor Age
Influences: Voices of Creative Dissent
New Town, Home Town

FREEDOM PRESS publish *Freedom* (fortnightly) and *The Raven* (quarterly) as well as books (more than sixty titles in print).

FREEDOM PRESS BOOKSHOP carries the most comprehensive stock of anarchist literature including titles from North America. Please send for our current list.

Freedom Press
in Angel Alley
84b Whitechapel High Street
London E1 7QX

TALKING
TO ARCHITECTS

ten lectures by
Colin Ward

FREEDOM PRESS
LONDON
1996

First published
by
FREEDOM PRESS
84b Whitechapel High Street
London E1 7QX
in
1996

ISBN 0 900384 88 3

Typeset by Jayne Clementson
Printed in Great Britain by Aldgate Press, London E1 7RQ

Contents

Foreword

This book is a gathering of lectures given to audiences, mostly of architects and town-planners over the past twenty years. Earlier collections published by Freedom Press, *Housing: An Anarchist Approach* (1976), *Talking Houses* (1990) and *Talking Schools* (1995) also include addresses to architectural audiences dating back to the early 1960s, when I moved out of earning my living in that particular industry.

I don't know how often other anarchists get asked to address audiences of nurses or doctors, solicitors or probation officers, engineers or plumbers, but for me the most interesting application of the nature-or-nurture debate concerns architects. Is a certain kind of person attracted to that profession or do the schools of architecture produce a particular kind of character? Alan Bennett reckons that he understands them, and provides an architect's profile in his book *Writing Home*: "grey hair, young face, bright tie and liberal up to a point (architects, like dentists, being the same the world over)."

My experience has been the opposite. It's an occupation that produces a wider range of practitioners than any other. I've met more anarchist, pacifist and socialist architects than dissident members of most jobs, professions or trades. For example, in 1995 a 78 year old graduate from Birmingham School of Architecture returned to Britain from India, for only the fourth time in fifty years, to gather an honorary doctorate from what is now the University of Central England.

He's Laurie Baker, who spent the war years working for the Friends Ambulance Service in China, and on the way home to pursue his real career, sought out Gandhi, while waiting for a ship in Bombay. The wily Mahatma recognised the kind of man whose approach to building meant using local materials and local labour to serve real needs. Baker has since been involved in at least a thousand low-cost projects based on vernacular building. He admitted to the *Architect's Journal* that, while besieged by potential clients, and while the government seeks his advice, he has "a very difficult relationship" with fellow professionals, adding that "everybody connected with the building industry is put on a percentage, so they think I'm crazy".

Exactly the same experience haunted his Egyptian equivalent, Hassan Fathy, whose personal history is described in the third of these lectures. He began, certainly, as an Alan Bennett stereotype, but rapidly learned that since his country's real assets were labour and mud, his work should be built upon these. Professional esteem came as late in life for Fathy as for Laurie Baker. Bad reputations spread widely, while good reputations stay local.

There are exceptions. For example, the late Walter Segal worked in obscurity for years until his simple yet subtle way of devising house-building techniques that anyone can use won him an immense reputation. He died a fulfilled and happy man. The fourth lecture in this book was a contribution to a symposium celebrating his achievement.

Similarly, there is the Italian advocate of "an architecture of participation", Giancarlo De Carlo, notably separated from the corrupt official system, who, in his seventies, is honoured by his fellow-architects around the world precisely for his lifetime of attempting to serve local community needs. When he came to London to receive the gold medal of the Royal Institute of British Architects, its president explained that De Carlo's work was "a testimony to community: he does not build monuments, he builds communities".

And in accepting the award, De Carlo talked about his first meeting with the anarchists in 1945: "I came to have a deep relationship with the group who published the journal *La Volantà* and, through them, the whole galaxy of Italian anarchism: exceptional people who have been the most important encounters of my life." In his address to the RIBA on 15th June 1993, he listed the writers who, he said, had shaped his view of the world. "They were Kropotkin, Godwin, Morris, Bakunin and Malatesta, Thoreau and Whitman, and of course Patrick Geddes."

His criticism of the architectural profession was for what he described as "the habit of taking the side of the powerful and leaving the weak to their fate". I agree. And, like him, I have watched a committed minority of them sticking to their social ideologies, finally winning recognition at the end of their lives. But how will the current generation of young committed architects ever pick up the work that will testify to *their* virtues? I've watched, and even examined, plenty of them and know very well about their skills and modest, sensible attitudes.

They're competent and aware, have served their time in unpaid technical aid, but aren't much good at the current self-promotional language of Mission Statements and Business Plans. If they work for existing practices, they find themselves doing jobs they despise. If they set up on their own, they are resigned to playing the tin-whistle in pubs or competently helping out at the local nursery school.

What they never get a chance to do is to practice their trade and design buildings for clients they respect. Hassan Fathy found that rich families in the Arab world wanted him to build for them with the techniques he wanted to provide for the poor. And Laurie Baker confesses that in India wealthy people approach him saying "I want a Laurie Baker house, no matter how much it costs!"

Architects are not at all the same the whole world over, but the ones whose work is important for you and me have the usual problem that nobody wants to employ them until they are too busy to want to be employed.

This collection of lectures explores not only the radical end of the architectural spectrum but the achievements which have been called 'architecture without architects'. For one of the paradoxes of the radical end of their profession is its insistence that, given just half a chance, people could build for themselves.

Colin Ward

1. *Alternatives in Architecture*

I don't suppose that there is anyone here who doesn't feel that we have an architecture of alienation, eminently visible here in Sheffield: the alienation between the designer, the maker, the product and the consumer. What joy does the physical setting of public life, industry, commerce, education, administration, leisure and housing give to the designer on the drawing-board, the operative on the site, the user of the building, or the passer-by with a seeing eye?

Now that the modern movement in architecture has spent its force, we can see that its ideological foundations were elitist or crudely mechanistic, that it ignored in the first place the environmental preferences of ordinary people, and in the second, the fact that modern bureaucratic systems, whether of the Western or the Eastern kind, would inevitably subvert the humane aspirations of architects, turning the professional either into computers producing packages or prima donnas producing jewellery. Yet there are, and always have been, alternatives.

The first is the vernacular alternative. Most of the world's buildings were not the result of the work of the professional architect. Everywhere, people built for themselves, using such locally available materials as were available to them. A decade ago Bernard Rudofsky's exhibition of *Architecture Without Architects* dazzled the visitor with its demonstration of the sheer perfection of the many forms that vernacular building had developed all round the globe, yet he told me last year

---

Lecture at Sheffield University Architectural Society, 11th February 1976.

that in the United States (it is less true of Britain) the teaching of architecture leaves no room for the study of unpedigreed, undated buildings. The monstrous growths, from Babylon to Brasilia, as Rudofsky put it, are all documented, what is left out is the ordinary, which is like restricting the science of botany to lilies and roses.(Vernacular architecture has never been homogenised, it can never be an international language, for it is rooted in places and their indigenous materials and patterns of life.) Its most disturbing feature for the business-man is its longevity, and its builders, Rudofsky emphasised, never thought of themselves as professional problem-solvers.

But it would be a mistake to suppose that it was produced by people who were naively unaware of the elements of design. J.M. Synge wrote of the Kerry peasantry that they "would discuss for hours the proportions of a new building – how high a house should be if it was a certain length, with so many rafters in order that it might look well ..."

In the West today, for an architect to design a vernacular building would (and does) simply result in Disneyland, but there are many countries where, just at the time when *we* are discovering the virtues of the still-extant vernacular tradition, considerations of prestige and status are leading to the adoption of Western-style high-technology building, using expensively imported materials and often providing a climatically unsuitable result. In Egypt, Hassan Fathy made heroic efforts to recreate the vernacular tradition, and produced structures which were cheap, efficient and beautiful, but could find no one in the ruling elite to support his activities. Indian architects like Charles Correa have had a similar experience. They want to use their understanding of traditional techniques for the poor, but only the rich can pay for it.

The vernacular is dead in the developed countries, though tribute is paid to it in neo-vernacular – or what Rudofsky would call volks-vernacular – buildings: the ranch-style house, etc. What may lead to the development of a new kind of vernacular tradition is the crisis of energy and resources.

So my second alternative is that of the ecological impulse. Contemporary building is distinguished by an extravagant energy input, because of the use of synthetic and highly-processed materials, because of the heavy use of power-plant on the site, and in terms of the continuous high level of power consumption in the working life of the building: permanent artificial lighting, heating and air-conditioning and mechanical services. The rising cost of energy and of raw materials will increasingly suggest the positive advantages of buildings which make fewer demands, especially in running energy costs.

This is a new factor in architectural thinking, although it would have been so obvious to our ancestors that they would not have needed to spell it out, and its implications are being studied at several levels. At one end of the scale is the study developed by Alex Gordon when he was president of the Royal Institute of British Architects, of Low Energy / Long Life / Loose Fit, and at the other are innumerable individual experiments in 'autonomous' housing using such devices as solar water-heaters, solar walls, wind generators, methane digesters, heat pumps, use of subsoil and other on-site materials. The research of this kind in the Department of Architecture in Cambridge (England) has as its objective "to devise a house with an integrated services system which is self-sufficient, making no demands on the centralised network system but at the same time providing a level of amenity similar to that currently enjoyed by the average householder".

On a wider scale is the attempt to devise an ecologically sound pattern of urban settlements as a whole. At either level the rediscovery of *constructional* methods of controlling the internal environment of buildings (for example, the 'bad-gir' or windscoop as a method of air-conditioning from Hyderabad) and the avoidance of materials whose original cost or processing cost would make their use prohibitive in the future, will lead to a new kind of architecture, as will the adaptation of existing structures.

And this leads me to my third, adaptive, alternative. Vernacular buildings waste nothing: they hate to destroy a structure, and will adapt the most unlikely buildings for new purposes. It is only a very few years since the orthodoxies of architecture encouraged the idea of throw-away buildings because most existing buildings had outlived their original uses. But this idea itself is by now more obsolete than the buildings to which it referred. Adaptability – which again was taken for granted by our ancestors – is an important criterion for an alternative architecture.

But an adaptable or malleable environment is important in another sense. The fully-finished *objet d'art* which was the aim of the great names of the modern movement (the environment designed to the last teaspoon and curtain by an architectural genius) relegates the occupier of the building to the role of caretaker. There is a school of thought among architects (for example, N.J. Habraken and Herman Hertzberger in the Netherlands) that seeks an architecture of alternative uses, which can be called in Ivan Illich's language *convivial*, because they give each person "the greatest opportunity to enrich the environment with the fruits of his or her vision" as opposed to those environments which deny this possibility to the user and, as Illich says, "allow their designers to determine the meaning and expectations of others".

A fourth way of looking at alternative architectures can be called the counter-cultural alternative. The official culture prescribes certain architectural forms: the individual one-family per house or apartment; the office beehive (luxury accommodation for the queen-bees, standard cells for the worker-bees); the giant factory complex (different entrances, canteens and lavatories for separate levels of the hierarchy); the huge educational institution; agro-industry on a vast scale, and so on.

The counter-culture postulates quite different building types: the multi-family house or commune; the reintegration of agriculture and industry and of brain work and manual work (in, for example, Kropotkin's *Fields, Factories and Workshops*, and the reflections on 'The New Commune' in Paul and Percy Goodman's *Communitas*); or the free school or college, which might be totally de-institutionalised, using the whole environment as an educational resource. Not only would the alternative culture prescribe quite different building forms, it would also combine them in quite different ways: the school which is also a workshop, the market-garden which is also an academy of music ...

For a fifth approach to alternatives, I have to turn to the populism of Simon Nicholson of the Open University, and his Theory of Loose Parts, to embrace the idea of an environment that can be shaped and re-shaped by its users. His Theory of Loose Parts claims that "In any environment, both the degree of inventiveness and creativity, and the possibilities of discovery, are directly proportional to the number and kinds of variables in it". This insight is closely linked to a sixth aspect of alternatives, the question of who is in control. We are fortunate that, once again, the principle has been very clearly stated, this time by the architect John Turner who, after years of experience in unofficial settlements in Latin America, set out precisely the concept of dweller control in the book he edited with Robert Fitcher, on *Freedom to Build* (Macmillan, 1972). As the publishers say on the cover of that book, "from their worldwide experience the authors show that where dwellers are in control, their homes are better and cheaper than those built through government programmes or large corporations". But their aim is not merely to save government money. They are concerned with personal and family fulfilment. Nor are they suggesting that their formula necessarily implies the owner-built house. But it does imply freedom from the exploitative or neglectful landlord. In new building, it does imply that, individually or collectively, the dweller should be his or her own general contractor. Nor does it necessarily mean doing without an architect. For example, one much-respected architect, Walter Segal, has, over the last ten years, been unlearning his previous assumptions and designing houses which achieve great economies by a meticulous use of stress-graded timber and of standard building components without any cutting to waste on the site. They are usually built by one or two carpenters who have become firm friends of his, with the help of the clients themselves. Current American experiences of 'sweat equity' and 'urban homesteading' are also relevant here.

And the reference to the particular skills of the building trades takes me to another nuance of the spectrum of alternatives, that I would call the syndicalist alternative. Bertolt Brecht asked one of the great questions of history in the poem that begins "Who built Thebes with its Seven Gates?" and goes on to wonder where the workers went when they knocked off for the day on the Great Wall of China.

Most of the monumental constructions of history were built by armies of slaves, and while the notion that the cathedrals of the Middle Ages were the product of dedicated bands of autonomous craftsmen is now regarded as a romantic myth (they were paid the current rate for a day's work), the very existence of this myth tells us how attractive is the idea of building as a communal activity, a cooperative enterprise in which the gap between designer and executant is closed, and in which the individual has pride of craft, skill and responsibility in the product.

Is it possible to create the kind of situation where this myth becomes true? And what effect would it have on actual buildings? There have been various attempts to change working relationships in the building industry itself. One example is that of the Building Guilds which had a brief life in England after the First World War, or the *sindicats de bâtiment* which exist to this day in France.

But from all these nuances of alternative approaches, I have to turn to the changing roles of architects themselves. The ethos behind their education and the assumptions behind the constitutions of their professional organisations is that the ethos of the architect is that of an independent professional. Actually a minority of architects, usually in small personal practices, rarely function in this way. Most are employed workers, either for other architects or for public authorities or private businesses. The majority of architects cannot be described as independent professional people, and the claims for specialised wisdom, judgement or expertise for the architect as 'leader of the building team' rest on assumptions that cannot be sustained.

Furthermore, the shift in the twentieth century in architectural training from pupilage or apprenticeship to university degree courses has been a matter of ensuring social status rather than of handing on professional wisdom. For example, John Turner asked 50-60 fourth and fifth year architectural students at the University of Morales in Mexico how many thought they would be earning a living as architects five years after graduating. None of them thought it likely, knowing that there was no effective demand for their services, nor for those of the 6,000 students of architecture in Mexico City alone.

At one time the architect's skill was considered to rest on his ability to manipulate the 'orders' of classical architecture, or the vocabulary of styles in general, or in the massing of volumes and spaces. These skills are irrelevant to all but a minute proportion of the designers of contemporary buildings. At one time, too, the architect was considered to be a 'master builder', but today is content to devote constructional and technical wisdom to specialists and technicians. If architects have a professional future at all, it is, in the phrase of Geoffrey Vickers, as "skilled understanders enabling people to work out their problems". This is not a matter for regret. I know several happy and fulfilled people who work in just this way, at the service of local community groups. Their reward is the friendship of everyone in the locality. Their problem is that of finding a free evening to pursue their own interests.

And if you ask them, they will tell you that the experience has transformed their lives. This is something that cannot be claimed through earning a living on the design of yet another new and unwanted speculative office block.

2. *The Future of the Design Professions*

My name is Colin Ward. I am the author of half a dozen books on housing and planning and associated themes like environmental education and vandalism. For many years, from the age of 16 to that of 40, I worked on the drawing board for several well-known firms of architects and planners. By chance my last architectural job, almost twenty years ago, was as Director of Research for the firm of architects responsible for the complex of buildings we are in today. I thus have considerable experience of the way design decisions are made.

The evidence I want to give is on three aspects of design. The first is on the professionalisation of design, the second is on the bureaucratisation of design and the third is on what I have chosen to call the narcissism of design.

About Professionalisation: The most uncomfortable part of the design professions' legacy from the Arts and Crafts movement is the notion that everyone is a designer, or that, in the language that Eric Gill inherited from William Morris, the artist is not a special kind of person, every person is a special kind of artist. They looked to a past in which professional designers, in their opinion, did not exist. They were right to the extent that most of the physical environment that survives from the pre-Victorian past, and that people flock to admire, was never touched by professional designers, except to destroy it. Architects themselves, bored with the

---

Evidence given in support of Mike Cooley at the Enquiry on the Future of the Design Professions, at the Barbican, London, 30th November 1983.

precepts of the modern movement which they imposed on the public for decades, are involved in what they call 'post-modernism', the major form of which is a style known as 'neo-vernacular' which is a back-handed compliment to the non-professional designers of the past.

Yet the restriction of the design professionals to the fact that we have, from experience, lost faith in them, has been to suggest that some improvement in their own education, a broader base, a higher standard of entry, a longer period of training, more research, more science, more computers, more knowledge, will put everything right. Most of us are familiar with the disastrously élitist effects of the Coldstream-Summerson reforms in art education, but let me cite the particular case of architecture. To be accepted for professional training involves at the outset three O Levels and two A Levels, preferably in the approved subjects, followed by six years of professional training, after which the successful aspirants find themselves preparing, say, window and door schedules for some building in the design of which they have had no part. Now within living memory – and I think you will probably agree that architectural standards were no lower aesthetically and slightly higher technically within the lifespan of some people still alive – it was totally different. Sir Clough Williams-Ellis confided to Sir Edwin Lutyens that he spent a term at the Architectural Association school learning his trade. "A term," said Lutyens, horrified. "My dear fellow, it took me three weeks." Well, I would ask people who flocked to the Lutyens Exhibition at the Hayward Gallery last year, or who are glued to the television to watch the re-run of *The Prisoner* for the sake of its setting in Williams-Ellis's architectural joke at Portmerrion, whether those two were better or worse architects than the people who by a restrictive Act of Parliament are today exclusively entitled to call themselves architects? I deliberately mention these architectural knights to indicate that I am not generalising from the experience of the riff-raff of the architectural profession, who all, no doubt, have been through the academic treadmill.

Professionalism *is* a conspiracy against laity, because the greater the expertise, the power and status of a profession, the smaller the opportunity for the citizen to make decisions. Ivan Illich, the most damaging of the new critics of the professionalisation of knowledge, remarks that:

It makes people dependent on having their knowledge produced for them. It leads to a paralysis of the moral and political imagination. This cognitive disorder rests on the illusion that the knowledge of the individual citizen is of less value than the 'knowledge' of science. The former is the opinion of individuals. It is merely subjective and is excluded from policies. The latter is 'objective' – defined by science and promulgated by expert spokesmen. This objective knowledge is viewed as a commodity which can be refined, constantly improved, accumulated and fed into a process, now called 'decision-making'. This new mythology of governance by the manipulation of knowledge-stock inevitably erodes reliance on government by people ... Over-confidence in 'better knowledge' becomes a self-fulfilling prophecy. People first cease to trust their own judgement and then want to be told what they know. Over-confidence in 'better decision-making' first hampers people's ability to decide for themselves and then undermines their belief that they can decide.

About Bureaucratisation: The comment I have just quoted is valuable because it links the process of professionalisation with that of bureaucratisation. For in the modern world professional design is a commodity which only the rich can afford, and this means wither business or government. In business the role of design is obvious to every consumer. It is that of inducing obsolescence by changing fashions of essentially the same produce by styling, and thus keeping the production lines rolling. The design ideology, inflating its role as usual, claims that it is concerned with the total product. The consumer knows that it's just a matter of changing the image, and has seen the streamlined-look, the rounded-corner-plastic-look, the rectilinear-teak-look, the two-tones-of-grey-look and the brushed-aluminium-look. Much more serious is the bureaucratisation of design in the public sector, where British firms of architects have felt competent to design everything from new cities in India to the organisation of hospitals in Canberra. Didn't their training and expertise make them world planners capable of planning anything in the world at the people's expense? They are also, of course, competent to design execution chambers for prisons in the gulf states. All part of the design brief.

In a highly centralised state like Britain, where design expertise has been put at the service of the bureaucracy, every error that would be trivial if it happened once, is multiplied a hundredfold when sanctified by the label 'design'. This is the lesson of the tower-block fiasco in housing. It is the lesson of the various consortia for school design, and it is the lesson of our experience of hospital design.

The Architects and Buildings branch of the Department of Education and Science used to have on its wall in its Poulson-designed headquarters outside Waterloo station a map of the country coloured according to the various design consortia it had persuaded local authorities to join. A white patch in the middle stood out as a reproach. This was Buckinghamshire, which in its reactionary way stood out against modern, rationalised, systematised school design. The map has gone now because fashions have changed. And Buckinghamshire, which went on building schools of brick, timber and tiles with non-leaking pitched roofs, finds that its buildings are cheap, simple and durable and that they got about 15% more school for their money through not following the bureaucratisation of design.

An exactly similar story could be told from the DHSS. William Tatton-Brown, who was the department's chief architect from 1959 to 1971, has concluded that the advice on hospital design which his department pushed out for years, was misguided. He claims in fact that nearly half (i.e. £1,500 million) of the public investment in hospital building in the 1970s has been mis-spent. Yet there is no area of architectural design in which more expertise and research has been invested than in that of hospital design. Tatton-Brown's conclusion, after his retirement of course, is quite significant. "Delegate responsibility as low down as possible" he said. "Give it to the people nearest to the patients".

I could tell a similar story about housing design, particularly with regard to the bureaucratisation of design in the LCC and its successor, the GLC, but I will move to my third objection to the design lobby.

The Narcissism of Design: The concentration of design in
the hands of professional designers has meant that, inevitably,
designers seek at all costs the approbation, not of their
anonymous clients, but of their fellow designers and, in
particular, that of those who are influential in the media of the
profession. This is why it has become almost axiomatic that
the kind of building that wins an award becomes one which is
loathed by the people who live or work in it. They just call
their school or office The Hothouse, or their block of flats
Alcatraz or Casablanca because it reminds them of the
vernacular architecture of penology or the forts of the French
Foreign Legion. In the new city of Milton Keynes there is a
quite measurable scale by which housing is assessed. At the
most disliked end of the scale comes the housing by the most
prestigious architects, the leaders of the profession. The most
sought after is that which most resembled the traditional
image of house-and-home, with a pitched roof and a chimney
on top and a front porch with roses round the door. This, of
course, is most despised by the design professions. The
highest praise that any council tenant can give his home is the
well-worn phrase 'it doesn't look like a council house'. This
is why the design professionals have the utmost contempt for
the people who are obliged to use their buildings.

There *are* alternative approaches to environmental design. I
have walked down the street in British towns with architects
who were greeted by everyone we met because they had been
enablers and not dictators. They had helped people to make
their own environment.

I am just like anyone else who has pondered for years on the
failure of the design professionals to serve, beyond a trivial
level, the needs of citizens. We need an alternative theory,
even one which denies that there *is* a future for the design
professionals in the sense in which we have known them in
the past. The best expression I have ever found of an
alternative approach was in a paper by Simon Nicholson,
which I published ten years ago in the *Bulletin of Environmental
Education*. He called it the Theory of Loose Parts, and he set
it out thus:

In an environment, both the degree of inventiveness and creativity and the possibility of discovery, are directly proportional to the number and kind of variables in it.

The argument he used to explain how he arrived at this principle is that the imposed environment, the one in which the citizen has a merely passive part to play, results from cultural elitism. He says:

Creativity is for the gifted few: the rest of us are compelled to live in environments constructed by the gifted few. We listen to the gifted few's music, use the gifted few's inventions and art, and read the poems, fantasies and plays by the gifted few. This is what our education and culture conditions us to believe, and this is a culturally induced and perpetuated lie.

Building upon this lie, the dominant cultural elite tell us that the planning, design and building of any part of the environment is so difficult and so special that only the gifted few – those with degrees and certificates in planning, engineering, architecture, art, education, behavioural psychology and so on – can properly solve environmental problems.

The result is that the vast majority of people are not allowed (and worse – feel that they are incompetent) to experiment with the components of building and construction. Whether in environmental studies, the abstract arts, literature or science, the creativity – the playing around with the components and variables of the world in order to make experiments and discover new things and form new concepts – has been explicitly stated as the domain of the creative few, and the rest of the community has been deprived of a crucial part of their lives and lifestyle.

We are groping both for a different aesthetic theory and for a different political theory. The missing cultural element is the aesthetic of a variable, manipulable, malleable environment: the aesthetic of loose parts. The missing political element is the politics of participation, of user control and of self-managing, self-regulating communities.

3. Drawing the Line: some dissident architects

I was immensely gratified when your college awarded me an honorary fellowship, and even hired me a gown to wear on the occasion, partly because I see it as a licence to pontificate, but also because in my years as an external examiner I have learned enormously from both staff and students here. The popular image of the architectural profession is either of a bunch of prima donna stars who luxuriate in the plum jobs or are slaves to private speculators or public bureaucracies. The minority dissident approach is to see architecture as a popular social activity, where the architect is an enabler, or fixer, rather than an aesthetic dictator. Most of these alternative advocates get invited to Hull, geographically and architecturally out on a limb, but which, because of its reputation, gathers students and teachers from all round the globe.

The long series of practitioners, including such people as John Turner, Nikolaas John Habraken, Charles Correa, Walter Segal, Giancarlo De Carlo and Hassan Fathy, who is the one I want to talk about tonight, all eventually get loaded with professional honours, but what they really want is for their approach to become the norm rather than an exception.

It is already 25 years since N.J. Habraken reminded us (in the book eventually translated as *Supports: An Alternative to Mass Housing*) that there was a time when every generation took it for granted than it could leave its own mark on building inheritance. In his view the urge to 'restore' old buildings

---

Lecture at Hull School of Architecture, November 1987.

increases in proportion to the decline of building as a *social* activity. And he saw this as a sign of the degeneration of building as a means of self-expression by the user:

> We cannot, moreover, draw the conclusion that the initiative to construct, improve or change is to be found only among the more affluent members of society. One has only to look at the backs of the poorer housing districts of some forty years ago. The quantity of extensions, balconies, pigeon lofts, sheds, conservatories and roof houses come ... as a relief to the observer who would rather see people than stones.

I am sure that this is one of the lessons in perception that plenty of people have absorbed at this school of architecture. I know this as an appreciative reader of dissertations here. As a historian, along with Dennis Hardy, of both 'plotlands' and holiday camps, I was prompted, for example by Phil Wren's dissertation on holiday shanties, to make a pilgrimage to Colley's Camp at Withernsea on the coast not far from here to test for myself his claim that even on a rainy day "the bright colours, neat gardens and painted fences make a gentle and poetic image in stark contrast to the alien atmosphere of the nearby modern chalet and caravan camps". He turned out to be right. As an observer of the way that children colonise an environment, I was drawn to Geoffrey Haslam's dissertation on 'Dens'. He recalled his own childhood succession of dens, hide-outs and camps, built with whatever materials came to hand. He then selected a group of people who seemed to him to be outstandingly creative in their adult lives and interviewed them about their childhood. He found that they had all been den builders and reflected on the building activities of children between the ages of seven and fourteen. He concluded that:

> ... considering that they can achieve so much at such an age with no assistance or guidance it seems odd that so few adults ever set about building even the simplest structure. Some time during their development, they lose the ability, confidence and motivation to build.

Together with David Crouch, I have written about the landscape and culture of allotment gardens, so we were especially interested in yet another Hull dissertation. Ray Garner studied one of the few instances where the *ad hoc* building urge *did* survive into adult life. His study of the allotment garden shed saw it as "probably Britain's most prolific and vigorous"

remaining example of the self-builder's art, precisely because
it had evaded the criteria of imposed controls on design:

The freedom is the abrogation of responsibility to the manners of
craftsmanship and aesthetics. 'Anything will do.' This separation from a
mechanical system and rules, together with a need to innovate, is the force
that clears the way for creativity and subconscious expression.

But of course, this school draws its students from all over the
world, from Africa, the Indian subcontinent, Latin America
and South-East Asia, for whom these marginal English
explorations are ... marginal. They know perfectly well, from
everyday familiarity, that over 90% of the world's dwellings
were built by their inhabitants without benefit of architects,
building firms or housing policy, using with incredible
ingenuity, the materials that came to hand, reeds, grasses,
bamboo and the elaborate technology of timber, or of mud,
adobe, stone or bricks, following the traditions of tribes, clans,
families or communes. They know too that today in the
squatter settlements of the world's exploding cities, the
buildings of the poor are constructed with the detritus of the
modern international economy, while those of the affluent,
and of the official and commercial world are constructed with
imported technologies and materials, as well as with imported
architectural and engineering expertise, and often even with
imported, contracted building work-forces.

They are familiar with architectural imperialism, and I have
seen here, many a project or dissertation concerned with the
possibilities and pitfalls of policies like 'Site and Services and
'Squatter Upgrading', or with the use of local technologies
instead of imported ones, in the building of health centres and
hospitals, primary and secondary schools.

This brings me to an event that happened last week in the
Old City of Cairo and to the architect I want to discuss. For
it was there that the American trade union, Bricklayers
International, presented an *architectural* award, the Louis
Sullivan Prize, to the 87-year-old architect Hassan Fathy. It
was a happy occasion for Fathy, partly because it came from
the United States, and he has always shared the view that the
rich nations have much to learn from the poor ones, and partly
because he has always attached importance to craft skills but

also on sharing them in the community. Years ago he stressed that "a man who acquires the solid mastery of any skill grows in self-respect and moral stature. In fact, the transformation brought brought about in the personalities of the peasants when they built their own village is of greater value than the transformation in their material conditions."

Fathy was born into a rich Egyptian land-owning family who spent their winters in Cairo and their summers in Alexandria, and were totally insulated from the lives of their fellow-countrymen. "Until my 27th year, I never set foot on any of our country property." When he did, he was doubly astounded, first by the serene beauty of the Egyptian rural landscape, and secondly by the appalling and degrading poverty of the villages of the *fellaheen*. How could he use his professional skill to enhance both?

He came to realise that mud, the only building material freely available to the peasants, was the material that would have to be used. Decades later he told the United Nations Habitat Forum in Vancouver, "There is no way out of it. People must build for themselves. *Not low-cost housing, but no-cost housing.*" In the 1930s his architectural practice began with country houses. "These houses, mostly for rich clients, were certainly an improvement on the old town type of country house, but largely because they were more beautiful. In spite of their economical mud brick wall, they were not so very much cheaper than houses built of more conventional materials, because the timber for the roofs was expensive."

The Second World War blocked supplies of imported building materials, but he reflected at the time that "Egypt has always imported steel from Belgium and timber from Romania, yet Egypt has always built houses". He would have to develop vaulted roofs. But vaults require wooden centring, as well as carpentry and masonry skills beyond the means of peasant builders. Fathy's first designs for vaulted dwellings, produced for the Royal Society of Agriculture, fell down. "It was clear that if the ancients had known how to build vaults without centring, the secret died with them".

Then he learned from his brother, an engineer at Aswan, that the Nubians still held the secret of building vaults which stood up under construction without any temporary supports. He hurried down to Nubia, full of anticipation. Aswan itself was a disappointment, "looking like a seedy Cairo transplanted to the country: the same pretentious facades, the same gaudy shop fronts, the same poor-relation, apologetic, would-be metropolitan air". But over the river, at Gharb Aswan, he found "a whole village of spacious, lovely, clean and harmonious houses, tall, easy, roofed cleanly with a brick vault, each house decorated individually and exquisitely around the doorway with mouldings and tracery in mud". It was, he wrote in his book *Architecture for the Poor*, "like a vision of architecture before the Fall: before money, industry, greed and snobbery had severed architecture from its true roots in nature".

His opportunity came when the Department of Antiquities was concerned about the village of Gourna on the site of the old cemetery of Thebes, across the river from Luxor. Many villagers made a living from tomb robbery, since ancient Egyptian artefacts were valued in the West. (They were, of course, a prey to the dealers who grew rich on this loot.) The site was to be taken over by the Department. This village of 7,000 inhabitants was to be rebuilt elsewhere, and the job of rehousing was to be entrusted to Fathy.

He developed a philosophy of village development and social reconstruction very like that of Gandhi and his followers like Vinoba Bhave and Jayaprakash Narayan in India: self-help, basic education, co-operatives, revived craft industries and public health measures to combat water-borne diseases like bilharzia. But there was dreadful bureaucratic opposition from the Department of Antiquities, and he tried in vain to interest more appropriate government departments. Work finally stopped, and Egyptian government architects for years afterwards dismissed the project as "a sentimental excursion along a byroad that could never lead to success".

Should he have waited for a revolution or at least for a new reforming regime? Well, the Farouk monarchy was finally overthrown, and there was the Neguib period, followed by Nasser's new Egypt with important land reforms, and the establishment of village co-operatives, as well as vast projects like the Aswan High Dam, but still no basic village development on the lines of New Gourna.

When Fathy revisited the place he found that the boys who had worked so eagerly in the craft school he had started were now young men – and unemployed. "Looking over the village with its deserted theatre, empty khan and craft school, and a few houses inhabited by squatters, with only the boys' primary school in use, I thought what Gourna might have been". The only things that flourished were the trees he had planted there, (perhaps because they were not subject to the administration) and the 46 masons who had been trained there.

In vain he sought a patron among the authorities in the New Egypt concerned with housing. "This is not to say that the authorities were not interested in the welfare of the people, but that an intrinsic incompatibility exists between the principles, aims and procedures of the co-operative system of building and those of the contract system, which is well established in the official economy and administration. I realised at last that I had to be my own patron if I wanted to continue with the struggle."

He has pursued a few more village projects whenever he got the chance in the Arab states, but the irony is that while the academic and bureaucratic elites have patronised European architects and their concrete, glass and steel, only the *cultural* élites have patronised him. The mud brick construction thought inappropriate for the poor has been adopted by rich clients who have been only too pleased to have astoundingly beautiful houses which enhance *their* environment.

Surrounded by cats and gleaned artefacts in his ancient apartment in the old City of Cairo, Fathy reflects that:

... the aspiring architect must unfortunately develop patience and a technique for working harmoniously with officialdom. Nevertheless, if solving architectural problems gives the satisfaction of climbing a mountain, co-operating with the bureaucracy is like wading through a bog – and soul-destroying, nothing less.

You will have heard similar conclusions from an assortment of alternative architects like Walter Segal, or from India, Charles Correa. But manipulating the system is one of the survival techniques we all have to learn.

Ten years ago, at the Town and Country Planning Association,

I was visited by the mayor of an Arabian city (an LSE graduate
and member of a princely house) accompanied by his Foreign
Office minder. He was visiting Britain to sound out various
firms of planning consultants. I, of course, remembered the
lecture that Fathy had given, not here, but at Essex University,
on "the Arab house in the urban setting: past, present and
future" in which he spelt out the implications of trusting in
professional solutions. In 1934, at the time of the second stage
of what we now have to call the Aswan Low Dam, when the
Nubians had to move, "35,000 homes were planned and
executed in one year by the peasants, without the assistance
of a single architect or engineer, for the low sum of 75,000".
When the region was flooded again in 1965 for the Aswan
High Dam, architects and planners moved this population
once more, building one identical house type. "To build just
half of the houses in this way cost £28 million."

So I told the mayor he was wasting his time coming to Britain
(pained look from the man from the Foreign Office). He
should have gone to Cairo and talked to Hassan Fathy. The
mayor threw back his head and laughed. "But he's mad," he
replied, "stuck there in the Old City!" Six months later I had
a letter from the mayor's office, thanking me for my courtesy
and naming the very well-known firm of British consultants
that had been appointed to advise him.

This is the kind of rebuff you can expect when you work in
the field of community architecture. And even your successes
will be muted by the sheer effort involved in accommodating
the official system of decision-making. It's a matter of learning
where to draw the line. My attitude, like that of Hassan Fathy
and many others, is like that expressed many years ago by the
American anarchist Paul Goodman. "A free man," he said,
(and of course he meant a free woman too):

... so long as he creates and goes by his clear and distinct ideas, can easily
maintain in his soul many apparent contradictions; he is sure they will iron
out; a loose system is the best system. But woe if at the same time he is
persuaded into prejudices and coerced into conforming: then one day he
will have the agony of drawing the line.

Well! there is a boyish joke I like to tell. Tom says to Jerry: 'Do you want
to fight? Cross that line!' and Jerry does. 'Now', cries Tom, 'you're on my
side!' We draw the line in their conditions; we proceed on our conditions.

4. Walter Segal: the go-between

My task as an anarchist is to say something about Walter's anarchist background, but to tell the truth, I know no more about this than he has told us in print. I would rather discuss him as a go-between: a link between separate worlds. In fact, he told us himself of his decision "to be and stay average in the no-man's land between Bohéme and Bourgeoisie".[1] He also explained the necessity of escaping from the milieu of his childhood into that of the village children in the Ticino, "so I had playmates in both camps which meant that I was affected by the lives of both the Bohemians and the ordinary philistines. And I have since found myself all the time moving from one camp to the other, never really able to adjust to one world only".[2]

So I have his own authority for describing him as a go-between. And in fact my own footnote in the Segal story is that of a go-between. He told me in the spring of 1976 that he was yearning to find a local authority willing to experiment in promoting self-build for families on its housing waiting list. He was wandering about the London Borough of Camden, since that was where the Segals lived. I advised against Camden simply because in my view (possibly wrong) the council was dominated by Labour Party ideologists whose idea of a socialist bliss was to have everyone a Camden council tenant. Secretly I had another reason. I was frightened that an approach by Walter would be given an instant and wounding brush-off simply because, in spite of his age and eminence, he

Lecture at the Symposium on Walter Segal at the Purcell Room, South Bank, London 7th June 1988.

would be seen as yet another architect touting for work. This I wanted to spare him.

I may have given him quite the wrong advice. For more than a decade later the London Borough of Camden is the only local authority, other than Lewisham, to have tried out the Segal method in putting up four relocatable buildings as housing for homeless families, built in eight weeks, I learn, "at one-third of conventional construction costs in inner London".[3] But at the time I thought that the London Borough of Lewisham was a better bet. This was for several reasons. One was that the chairman of its housing committee at that time was a highly intelligent comprehensive school head teacher Ron Pepper. Another was that the chairman of the planning committee was the idiosyncratic Nicholas Taylor, who knew the borough better than any of its staff through endlessly surveying it by bicycle. But the most important reason was that the recently appointed deputy borough architect was a dear anarchist friend of mine, Brian Richardson, a refugee from Kent County Council's architects' department as he declined to adopt its then favourite system for school building.

Now Harriet, my wife, has her birthday on the 8th of July and when we lived in London had the very nice habit of a big party on the nearest Saturday. We plotted to bring the Segals and the Richardsons together. Walter and Moran came, and up from Kent by motorcycle came Maureen and Brian Richardson. Well of course they were on the same wavelength and everything else followed, in spite of endless and agonising delays, which, however bad they were for Walter and Brian, were even worse for the Lewisham self-builders. Lewisham's housing committee had decided by one vote to give the proposal a chance. I was interested to learn a few weeks ago in a charming recollection by Nicholas Taylor in the *Architects' Journal* how two years earlier he had refereed an unsuccessful meeting between Walter and John Hands, then of Student Co-operative Dwellings in one corner and "an elderly and uncomprehending development control planner" in the other. Taylor recalls that "Walter's suicidal enthusiasm had certainly softened me up".[4] So my advice was right. Though none of us thought so two years later when that poor little enterprise at Lewisham was bogged down in labyrinthine bureaucratic tangles far beyond the five months it took to get planning permission from Lewisham, involving the GLC, the district surveyor, the Department of the Environment and even the Inland Revenue.[5] A sad illustration of the anarchist contention that government is a confidence trick by which citizens pay for being prevented from initiating anything.

That was the sum total of my own role as a go-between. I must now turn back over a century to 1872 when a celebrated aristocratic Russian geographer, Peter Kropotkin, made his first visit to Western Europe. Like all Russians he went first to Switzerland, intoxicated by the air of a democracy, even a bourgeois one. Zurich was full of Russian students, living on bread, tea and talk. In Geneva he was urged to go on to Sonvilier, a valley in the Jura hills, where the watch-case makers had, with the workers of the Neuchâtel area, formed the Jura Federation of disciples of the Russian anarchist Michael Bakunin. One of the watchmakers, Adhemar Schwitzguebel, with whom Kropotkin was later closely associated, took him into their home workshops. It was the turning-point in his life, beautifully described in his autobiography,[6] though for brevity I will read you the account by a biographer, Martin Miller:

Kropotkin's meetings and talks with the workers on their jobs revealed the kind of spontaneous freedom without authority or direction from above that he had dreamed about. Isolated and self-sufficient, the Jura watchmakers impressed Kropotkin as an example that could transform society if such a community were allowed to develop on a large scale. There was no doubt in his mind that this community would work because it was not a matter of imposing an artificial 'system' such as Muraviev had attempted in Siberia but of permitting the natural activity of the workers to function according to their own interests. He was further impressed in Sonvilier by the prevailing influence of Bakunin, whose name was invoked more as a moral influence than as an intellectual authority. All of these observations brought Kropotkin to the point of disrespecting all authority and uncritically worshipping the downtrodden masses. It is at this juncture that he dates his conversion: 'I became an anarchist'.[7]

Kropotkin returned to Russia, was involved in underground agitation, was imprisoned in the Peter-Paul Fortress, escaped to England, returned to Switzerland, where he recalled:

"When I was in Switzerland I could say that during my three or four years' stay in the country I was acquainted with none but workers". He was expelled, even from that country, and imprisoned in France before settling first in Harrow, and then at Viola Cottage in Bromley, Kent, before returning to Russia in 1917. Now the particular independence of mind, literacy and eager discussion of everything from first principles that he admired in the Jura peasant-craftsmen was similarly noted in the Ticino, the Italian-speaking canton, by the celebrated writer Francesco Chiesa. He recalls how "the shepherds, who spent the summer in the Alps, came down from time to time to restock with supplies, and these were bread, wine, salt and newspapers. And in some of their thatched huts up there, like so many troglodytes, in the acrid smells of curdled milk, smoke and dung, more than once I have happened to find them discussing the last minute detail of cantonal and world politics, with me addressing them in dialect while they took care to reply in the literary language".[8] It was just like Kropotkin's experience in the Jura: "I was asked to take a seat on a bench, or table, and soon we were all engaged in a lively conversation upon socialism, government or no government, and the coming congresses".[9]

Kropotkin's account of the wisdom and capacity of 'ordinary' people in 1872 can be paralleled by Walter's recollection in 1982 of the lessons of Lewisham. He said:

Help was to be provided mutually and voluntarily – there were no particular constraints on that, which did mean that the good will of people could find its way through. The less you tried to control them the more you freed the element of good will – this was astonishingly clear. Children were of course expected and allowed to play on the site. And the older ones also helped if they wished to help. That way one avoided all forms of friction. Each family were to build at their own speed and within their own capability. Which meant that we had quite a number of young people in their twenties and late twenties. But we had some that were sixty and over who also managed to build their own houses. They were told that I would not interfere with the internal arrangement. The time it has taken me not to be the normal hectoring architect that lays down everything and persuades everybody to follow his own taste. I let them make their own decisions, therefore we had no difficulties. What I found astonishing with these people was the direct personal friendly contact that I had with them and which they had among themselves. And quite beyond that the tapping of their own ideas – countless

small variations and innovations, and additions were made by them which
we have not yet tabulated because the whole thing was not sufficiently
organised. But it is astonishing that there is among the people that live in
this country such a wealth of talent.[10]

It is just like Kropotkin impressed by an "example that could
transform society if such a community were allowed to develop
on a large scale". And it took a lifetime in the wilderness to
rediscover that lesson. I put it this way because another virtue
of Nicholas Taylor's little comment is that he stresses that we
are celebrating an architect whose practice was singularly
small in output, even allowing for the fact that he insisted on
being a genuine professional in operating a one-man business.
Taylor says, "in past centuries, people like Walter were burnt
as heretics or marginalised as court jesters, and marginal
indeed was his place in the Modern Movement until he was
almost 70".[11] And the very revealing catalogue of his works
compiled by Philip Christou[12] only needs comparing with the
output of housing and schools in the post-war decades from
well-connected left-wing architects known to us all, who
would not dream of putting up little buildings in Hackney for
the Premium Pickle Company or a little office for Tretol Ltd
and a few self-generated housing projects. "It became clear to
me," he recalled, "that one can have a small path and tread it
alone".[13]

Now to go back to Ticino with its mountains and lakes. It
wasn't populated solely by Francesco Chiesa's literate
shepherds. North Europeans seem irresistibly drawn to the
sunny south in search of physical, spiritual or moral health.
Walter tells us that "in 1900 Henri Oedenkoven, a Fleming
from Antwerp, had founded a colony in which he and his
confederates tried to find a new meaning of life". This was
Monte Verità, the Mountain of Truth in the hills above
Ascona, and other sources tell us that the co-founder was Karl
Gräser from the German minority in Hungary, whose younger
brother Gustav was met wandering through Germany with
"long hair, sandals and bare legs" by the writer Hermann
Hesse, who immediately followed him down to Ticino, where
Hesse was to spend most of his life.[14] Monte Verità has its
place in history precisely because, just as Walter says, several

of the writers, painters and revolutionaries who stayed there later became world-famous. His own characterisation of the place is well-known: "The colonists abhorred private property, practised a rigid code of morality, strict vegetarianism and nudism. They rejected convention in marriage and dress, party politics and dogmas: they were tolerantly intolerant".[15] Tales do expand with the telling, and Walter's account contains errors. For example he says that one visitor was "the anarchist and poet, Erich Mühsam, who later lost his life tragically in fighting for his cause in 1918 in Munich". In fact it was Gustav Landauer who was murdered by an army officer in 1919. Mühsam was imprisoned and in 1934 was killed by the Nazis at Orienburg.[16] Perhaps Landauer too was at Monte Verità. Histories of the place do exist, but I have never been able to lay hands on one.[17]

I must now turn to the Kropotkin connection. We learn from Philip Christou that Walter was born at Berlin-Charlottenburg, son of Arthur and Ernestine Segal, in 1907 and lived from 1914 to 1918 at Ascona, and from 1918 to 1920 at Matten, near Interlaken. The Monte Verità years were thus when he was aged about seven to eleven. His father, an expressionist painter was a friend of Oedenkoven's, and his benefactor and his own first client, for the Casa Piccola, was Bernard Meyer. I wish I had had the time to find out more about this man. By Walter's account he was "a peasant's son who became a millionaire and fanatical anarchist with a guilt complex about money. A friend of Kropotkin's during the latter's stay in Switzerland, he had founded an anarchist community at Rapperswyl on the Zurich Lake ... and he supported and assisted countless people with a cause to fight for, though he never ceased to rebuke them for not joining the anarchist movement".[18] In his absorbing essay on Segal, John McKean tells of a visit to the Villa Bernardo at Ascona, because the Casa Piccola stands in its grounds: "Meyer's daughter, now an old lady, was having her siesta when the grand-daughter showed us in. There was a call from upstairs. In German she shouted up 'It's a friend of the son of the painter Segal, mother; they would like to see the son's little house".[19]

I would certainly like to know more about Meyer, and to separate truth from legend. Swiss anarchism has produced an absorbing variety of twentieth century anarchist characters, from Bertoni to Brupbacher, but I'm well aware that one of the anarchist vices is *papyrophilia*, the desire to bury oneself in mounds of old paper. I just asked the historian Heiner Becker about Meyer, and he replied that the man's fortune was made in the fur trade and that he lived in Brussels until one day, round about 1908, he was held up by a group of anarchist 'illegalists', who had the worthy, Robin Hood, desire to rob the rich to feed the poor. Such people usually choose those of the rich who sympathise with the cause rather than those who surround themselves with security police. They took a lot of money off him at gun-point, and he resolved to leave Brussels forever and settle in his native Switzerland. Thus it was that in Walter's childhood, "We lived in abject poverty until one day a short and powerfully built man came, looked at the paintings and asked my father how much he needed to live on. My parents thought about 300 francs a month was the family's budget and the visitor undertook to be responsible for this; indeed he continued for nearly thirty years".[20]

Walter's autobiographical fragments show that he went on to an orthodox European secondary education and that he very consciously sampled what was on offer in architectural training. I'm one of those people to whom he declared that his real good luck was when he picked up a book about the American tradition of house-carpentry in home and barn. I have frequently met people reared in self-consciously libertarian households who just yearned to be like all the other kids, just as I have met plenty of that majority who have spent a lifetime escaping from their parents' automatic authoritarianism. I think he reached an absolutely balanced view of this, with his remark that "To have spent childhood and adolescence in an environment of artists, architects, writers, life-reformers, thinkers and truth-seekers, ideologues and mystics, charlatans and cranks, many of whom have left their mark upon our time – and unfortunately perhaps, continue to do so – was in a way a singular piece of good luck; but there were moments when I longed for ordinariness and went to seek it".[21] But there is another side to this. Peter Blundell Jones is quite right in saying that "at Monte Verità Walter saw enough artistic self-indulgence to last a lifetime", but he is also right in perceiving that "Walter was already steeped in far too rich and broad a culture and had become too much of a lone wolf ever to join any pack. He had to find his own way in everything, and confessed that he could never submit to authority".[22]

He really was a go-between, poised in the middle of the world of revolutionary theorists and that of pragmatic people who just wanted to get on with the next job, on time, within the client's budget and giving satisfaction. I'm a known anarchist, and though I remember him being very kind about my books, the only time anarchism came into any conversations we had was in the form of quips about anarchists actually doing what they said they would do, on time. Brian Richardson tells me that, long into the night, he discussed every conceivable subject with Walter on the assumption that there was no need to get through the demolition of authoritarian prejudices: they could begin on common ground.

For Brian and for Ken Atkins, Walter was quite obviously a natural anarchist, and one who lived his anarchism more than most. I'm a little hesitant to claim him as an anarchist, simply because I don't think that's the way he saw himself. I see him as an intransigent individualist, thinking everything out from first principles and anxious to protect himself from ideology, politics and great events.

Now there's one thing significantly absent from any published account of Walter's life and utterances or writings. It's open to you to correct me if I am wrong. There is no mention of the mutual slaughter that was happening among the nations north of Switzerland in the years 1914-1918 when the Segal family were resident in Ascona. Nor is there any mention of the events of 1939 to 1945, or even of the events in Germany from the election of the National Socialist German Workers Party in 1933. Walter had the good sense to come to this country from Egypt in 1934, and to stay. We just don't know, though we can guess what happened to many other Segals from Berlin-Charlottenburg. You may think that in raising this taboo issue I am somehow criticising Walter for not being part of what used to be called the 'anti-fascist struggle'. For all I know he was. I believe that just as he had quite early in life had his fill of artistic self-indulgence, so he had seen enough of grand political gestures. I think Peter Rich was right in his tribute after Walter's death when, describing him as a born outsider, he noted how "from a position outside the various clans, magic circles and fashionable groupings he developed a powerful independent critical awareness. This in turn allowed him to free himself from one *tyranny* [his word] after another – from neckties, jackets, styles, wet trades, quantity surveyors, the list is endless. Given his warm personality this insight goes some way to explain his ever outstretched helping hand to anyone finding themselves temporarily with him on the outside".[23] But of course that very outstretched hand made him not so much an outsider as a go-between.

References

1. Walter Segal, 'Timber Framed Housing' in *RIBA Journal*, July 1977.

2. Walter Segal, 'Into the Twenties' in *Architectural Review*, January 1974.

3. 'Shacking Up' in *Architects' Journal*, 16th September 1987.

4. Nicholas Taylor 'Learning the Lewisham Way' in *Architects' Journal*, 18th May 1988.

5. 'Segal self-build hits bureaucratic chaos' in *Architects' Journal*, 16th August 1978.

6. Peter Kropotkin, *Memoirs of a Revolutionist*, 1899. Modern editions are those edited by Nicolas Walter (Dover Publications, 1971) and edited by Colin Ward (Folio Society, 1978).

7. Martin A. Miller, *Kropotkin* (University of Chicago Press, 1976).

8. Freely translated from the superscription to Jonathan Steinberg, *Why Switzerland?* (Cambridge University Press, 1976).

9. Kropotkin, *op. cit.*

10. Walter Segal 'View from a Lifetime' in *Transactions of the RIBA*, Volume 1, 1982.

11. Nicholas Taylor, *op. cit.*

12. *Architects' Journal* Special Issue on Walter Segal, 4th May 1988.

13. Walter Segal, *Architectural Review*, January 1974.

14. Ralph Freedman, *Hermann Hesse: Pilgrim of Crisis* (Jonathan Cape, 1979) and Volker Michels *Hermann Hesse: Sein Leben in Bilden und Texten* (Suhrkamp Verlag, 1979).

15. Segal *op. cit.*

16. See *Anarchy 54*, August 1965 on Buber, Landauer and Mühsam.

17. For example see Robert Landmann, *Monte Verità, Ascona. Die Geschichte eines Berges*, 3rd edition (Ascona: Pacaldi Verlag, 1934).

18. Walter Segal, *Architectural Review*, January 1974.

19. John McKean 'Semi preziosi di buon senso' / 'Lift High the Roofbeams, Carpenters' in *Spazio e Società*, No 34, June 1986. (This issue also contains a shortened version in English and Italian of Walter Segal's 'Monte Verità and the '20s' from his lecture printed in the *Architectural Review*, January 1974.) McKean's essay is reprinted in *Building Design*, 20th May 1988.

20. Information from Heiner Becker, International Institute of Social History, Amsterdam, and from Segal *Architectural Review*, January 1974.

21. Segal *op. cit.*

22. Peter Blundell Jones in *Architects' Journal*, 4th May 1988.

23. Peter Rich 'Walter Segal: Notes on a Friendship' *AIII Times*, Autumn 1985.

5. 'A wonderful place to grow up in'

I am honoured to be asked to deliver the first Cornelis van Eesteren lecture. But today *is* World Town Planning Day, originated in France but celebrated in Buenos Aires and other cities, whose planning problems make those of countries like the Netherlands or Britain seem simple. It is a reminder to us that popular direct action among poor people in cities like Bogota, Caracas or Mexico City, has developed an unplanned city from below which has integrated the unofficial economy, the unofficial housing, welfare and transportation systems into the cities whose public planning system was unwilling to accept those huge pressures from below. People make their own cities.

This subversive thought leads me to the particular aspects of Cornelis van Eesteren's ideas and influences that I want to discuss today. I learn from the account of his life by Franziska Bollerey that even his address-book "is an odyssey through the architectural and cultural history of our time", and I take my title from a remark Professor Bollerey about the place where he was born. Talking about the village of Kinderdijk-Alblasserdam, he described it as "A wonderful place to grow up in".

Now every single person here would like her or his children to reflect upon their childhood home as 'a wonderful place to grow up in'. Could we say that *this*, and not any considerations of how planning relates to the prospects of the particular place

The first Cornelis van Eesteren Lecture to the Netherlands Society of Urban Planners, at Delft University, 8th November 1990.

of the Netherlands or Britain, or any other national economy in the integrated European market, is what matters to us as citizens of anywhere? A wonderful place to grow up in is what every parent wants, and this is *not* guaranteed by performance in international markets. If it were, tourists from rich countries like yours or mine would not be flocking to the poor countries of the world to spend their holidays admiring the remains of ancient cultures which have been destroyed by *our* worship of the economics of the market.

I want to concentrate on just two aspects of van Eesteren's odyssey through the cultural history of our time. The first has to do with his life-long friendship with Arthur Müller-Lehning, secretary of the anarcho-syndicalist international, and later editor of the *Archives Bakounine* from the International Institute of Social History in Amsterdam. This was an important link, not only with the Dutch anarchist tradition of people like Domela Nieuwenhuis, and later Albert de Jong and Bart de Ligt, but with the whole international anarchist stream of Proudhon, Bakunin, Kropotkin and Malatesta.

But what has this by-way among van Eesteren's widespread cultural interests to do with your conference's theme of Urban Design in the twenty-first century? The connection is historically closer than we might imagine. You will be as familiar as I am with the work of the much-travelled urban geographer Peter Hall, who has enjoyed your hospitality as much as I do. He opens his new book *Cities of Tomorrow*, which is a history of twentieth-century planning ideas, with a section in which he unravels what he describes as the *anarchist* roots of the planning movement.

Professor Hall returned to this theme exactly a year ago when he came to London to address a meeting of exactly the same kind as the one which brings us together today. It was the 75th anniversary conference of the Royal Town Planning Institute, and he declared that:

... there has been a very general groundswell in the last five years in favour of what could be called the neo-anarchist tradition of planning: the tradition that goes directly back to Patrick Geddes and Ebenezer Howard, and behind them to their spiritual teachers, Peter Kropotkin and Michael Bakunin and Pierre-Joseph Proudhon.

He was addressing, just as I am, an audience of professional planners and urban designers, and I do not know whether they agreed with him or even understood the tradition to which he was referring so optimistically. But Cornelis van Eesteren would have understood, since for him Ebenezer Howard's work was one of *the* classics of town planning, while Franziska Bollerey tells us that the dictum of Patrick Geddes, "Survey before plan" was central to his approach: "When van Eesteren repeatedly pointed out '*Nous avons éxaminé, nous avons trouvé*', he refers exactly to this thesis".

And this leads me to the second aspect of van Eesteren's journey through the cultural history of his century, closely associated with the first. It has great relevance to any consideration of the year 2015, much more, in fact,than the endless technical fantasies about the future of cities that have punctuated our own century. We yawn at yet more prophecies of mile-high skyscrapers, tower blocks with helicopter landing pads on the roof, automated and metered urban motorways, or plastic domes covering the whole city.

They bore us because they fail to address the real issues that concern us, whether in housing, transport, employment, aesthetics or the rescue of the environment. These are not technical problems. As van Eesteren insisted, "Design is a question of ethics and morality". Nor do technical solutions affect our belief that the citizens themselves should shape the future of the places where they live and work and rear their children, for whom we want 'a wonderful place to grow up in'.

At the end of the last century, in the days when town-planning was thought of as a social movement, not a profession, there were three remarkable prophets of the dilemmas that face us today and will still face us in the year 2015.

The first, of course, was Ebenezer Howard, whose book from 1898, *Garden Cities of Tomorrow* provided us with those simple little diagrams that have become the shorthand of regional planning everywhere. The second was the remarkable Scotsman, Patrick Geddes, organiser of the first town planning exhibition, whose work was put into perspective for all of us by Lewis Mumford. The third was Peter Kropotkin, the Russian geographer and anarchist, whose book *Fields, Factories and Workshops*, also published in 1898, was, just as Mumford noted, half a century in advance of contemporary economic and technical opinion in grasping that the flexibility and adaptability of electric power would make the giant industrial city obsolete, would facilitate rapid transit and communication, and *could* ensure the viability of small-scale horticulture combined with a small-workshop economy, just as it *could* enable us, in both our working lives and our social lives, to combine brain work with manual work.

These three thinkers *might* have shared the ideology of town and country planning, just as Peter Hall suggested, but for the fact that there were other, far more powerful trends. I think it is quite important for me to stress that these three men would not have qualified for membership of the Royal Town Planning Institute in Britain, nor of the American Planning Association, nor indeed of the Netherlands Society of Urban Planners. Except, perhaps, Kropotkin, whose original reputation was as a geographer. As for Howard, he was a stenographer, while Geddes was a marine biologist.

I find it endlessly interesting that these founding fathers thought of planning, *not* as a profession nor as a body of legislation, but as a popular movement, a public enthusiasm, part of the *social* economy. Can we have socially-efficient, and consequently energy-efficient cities? Kropotkin argued, in his *Fields, Factories and Workshops* that "political economy, as it gradually emerges from its semi-scientific stage" tends to become a science devoted to the study of human needs "and of the means of satisfying them with the least possible waste of energy".

And he claimed that "the main subject of *social* economy – that is, the *economy of energy required for the satisfaction of human needs* – is consequently the last subject which one expects to find treated in a concrete form in economical treatises". When that book was reprinted just after the First World War, a new introductory note explained that it "pleads for a new economy in the energies used in supplying the needs of human life, since these needs are increasing and the energies are not inexhaustible".

In those days no-one else was talking in such terms, but this, is precisely the issue that *should* be dominating our reflections on the future of cities.

Patrick Geddes too, was in advance of everyone else in believing that the most important thing about planning was the participation of the citizens. His book *Cities in Evolution*, written in the years leading up to the First World War (when Britain, following the example of the Netherlands, had just introduced its first town planning legislation) was really a handbook on environmental education and the involvement of the people who live and work in any place in environmental decision-making. When the British planner Jacqueline Tyrwhitt re-edited that book, over forty years ago, she observed that:

Geddes was not greatly preoccupied with the training of the expert. He was far more concerned that the ordinary citizen should have a vision and a comprehension of the possibilities of his own city. Thus Geddes lays all his emphasis on the need for a Civic Exhibition and a Permanent centre for Civic Studies in every town – an Outlook Tower (like the one he created in Edinburgh). This is something that, with all our discussions on the need for the value of 'citizen participation' in town planning, has yet to be given a trial.

It was Geddes who urged us to see the city in its regional setting, and who argued that planning is "the development of a local life ... capable of improvement and development in its own way and upon its own foundation, not something which can be done from above, on general principles easily laid down, which can be learned in one place and imitated in another". His approach to urban management adopted a completely decentralist standpoint. In 1912 he declared that "for fulfilment there must be a resorption [the word he was looking for was re-absorption] of government into the body of the community. How? By cultivating the habit of Direct Action instead of waiting upon representative agencies".

This is the opposite of contemporary trends in 1990. But what about the year 2015? Will we have moved further away from, or closer to, local decision-making? I need to remind you that below all the political talk of a Europe of the *nations*, there is a growing undercurrent looking forward to a Europe of the *regions*, where the nation-state becomes an anachronism, not because national powers are surrendered to a trans-national or supra-national authority but in favour of regional and local autonomy. (Like the rest of Europe I am out of step with Mrs Thatcher!) I look forward to the Switzerisation of Europe, not through admiration of Switzerland, but because I believe that regionalism and localism is the necessary concomitant of federalism.

Geddes had yet another legacy for us. He had a message, seventy years ago, for anyone who believes that future populations can be *confined* in the city. "I have to remind all concerned", he said, "first that the essential need of a house and family is *room*, and secondly that the essential improvement of a house and family is *more room*". He was accurately predicting a trend which has preoccupied planners and housing authorities all through the twentieth century, and which is certainly going to persist into the twenty-first. We all demand more domestic space.

In 1904, Geddes read a paper on 'Civics as Applied Sociology' at the London School of Economics. The man who rose to open the discussion was Ebenezer Howard, the author of *Garden Cities of Tomorrow* and the draughtsman of its illustrations which included the most famous planning diagrams in the world. One was his picture of The Three Magnets and the other was his vision of The Social City.

Howard stood up and said that "while the age in which we live is the age of the great closely-compacted, overcrowded city, there are already signs, for those who can read them, of a coming change so great and so momentous that the twentieth century will be known as the period of the *great exodus*".

Now this was a prophecy that certainly came true. The demographic statistics of the whole of western Europe and the United States show that Howard was right in his prediction. This outward movement from the overcrowded city has happened all through this century and is certainly going to continue into the next. Howard offered an alternative to the prospect of endless suburbanisation by his advocacy of the Social City. He called it a 'Group of Slumless Smokeless Cities' and his famous diagram showed them linked by an 'Inter-Municipal Canal' and an 'Inter-Municipal Railway'. And as we all know, he built his two demonstration models in the form of Letchworth and Welwyn Garden Cities, to show what the constituents of his polynuclear social city could be like.

Belatedly, after decades of propaganda and lobbying, some of his ideas became public policy in the British government's programme of New Towns after the Second World War. But of course, many of Howard's proposals were lost or forgotten on the way: in particular his insistence that the new cities should be the common property of their inhabitants, and that the increase in land values should belong to them, and not to property speculators, to be used for their common, co-operative purposes.

In the jargon of geographers, Howard, like Geddes and like Kropotkin, was imagining a polynucleated city region, and his Social City diagram had a Central City (even though a small one) at its heart. So planners in Britain saw London, or Birmingham or Glasgow as the central city, with a ring of new towns, separated from it by a Green Belt.

In real life the central city has remained dominant, and its associated hinterland has become the commuter city. The affluent can leap over the Green Belt, living in old towns and villages beyond it, while the poor are trapped in what in Britain and America is described as an 'Inner City ghetto', which more often than not is to be found, not in the gentrified inner city, but in its bleak, poverty-stricken municipal housing estates on the periphery.

It is in adapting the urban fabric to the realities of the Social City, that, as you all know, the rest of the world envies the Netherlands, just because in Randstad, Holland, you have the world's one genuine polynucleated city region. In adapting to the world of 2015, you see the problems. We see the huge advantages you have inherited from history: a social city without the disadvantages inherent in a central city: a Greenheart City with the energy-saving blessing of an environmentally friendly transport system. Potentially, at least!

Countries like Britain or France, with a history of centralised despotic autocracy in which London or Paris was the seat of the monarch, the government, public administration, business, finance, and also the heart of the communication systems, have found it hard to adapt to the realities of dispersed city regions. The Netherlands, with a history rooted in the free cities of the Middle Ages, (beautifully celebrated by Kropotkin in his classic study of *Mutual Aid*), found it much easier to adapt to modern realities.

I know that you are gloomy about the endless pressures of expansion that make the cities around the ring spread across the buffer zones into one urbanised mass, or of the continual urbanisation of the rural centre itself. But you are tackling your problems. In Britain they are being ignored because of a primitive faith in market forces. Yours are nothing compared with the ones that contemporary Britain declines to face: the dominance of London and the ever-expanding South-Eastern region and of a transport system that, whether by road, rail or air, is concentrated upon the central city.

Now if we project our decentralist vision into the twenty-first century, with a new consciousness of resources, energy-saving, global warming and pollution, and all the other issues on our crowded agenda, we all face similar problems. The Netherlands government, like the British, envisages an expanding European economy with its own industry's increasing national share. Some nations, somewhere, are going to be disappointed. A minority of serious people everywhere, think about the enormous problems, which affect our personal budgets and aspirations, of how we can make the huge leap to a sustainable future economy.

It does not need much of a flight of the imagination to foresee that by the year 2015, all political parties in every European country will be green parties. But they will be advocating different shades of green. For example there will be public relations campaigns to assure us that any particular entre-preneurial activity is justified because it generates employment and conquers new markets, thus generating the income to pay for our expensive anti-pollution measures.

At the other extreme of the spectrum there will be *misanthropic* greens. I chose this word, since it means 'haters of humans' because in rich countries like the United States there are already people who, in their support of the natural world, hate their fellow-humans for intruding on it.

In between these two attitudes there is a very common one, known by the acronym of *NIMBYism*, meaning Not In My Backyard. This is endemic in both the United States and

Britain, so it must be in the Netherlands too. It says 'I have built a house in the forest, or converted an ancient piggery or barn into a desirable residence, and I am determined that no-one else shall intrude on the view of fields, woods and trees that I see from my bedroom before I go to work in the city in my Audi'.

Professional planners, whether their concern is with land use or with urban design, will, as servants of the community, find their task increasingly difficult. But what does the community demand? I myself have known people who at the age of 21 had left the suffocation of their parents' suburban home, and were waiting for the revolt of the proletariat in the city, and who at the age of 31 were praising God and growing beans in the countryside. The problem is that when they are 41 they are back in the city, working as consultants, and propagating the view that it is axiomatic that we should live at high densities and walk to work. At 51 they are back in the suburbs, rearing a second family and waiting for early retirement.

One of the things this teaches us is that our most precious environmental possession, and the one which we lose least willingly, is mobility, whether this means personal, social, occupational or ideological mobility. Humans change. And their changing needs are not arbitrary. There are different habitats that they see as appropriate to changing roles in the family life cycle, quite apart from changes in the means of livelihood or employment. The one kind of mobility that can be planned for as a social good for everyone is the simplest kind: transport: the Freedom to Go.

Now your ancestors and mine, the canal-builders in the eighteenth century, discovered that a single horse could move two tons on a level road, ten tons on rails and eighty tons by water. Water transport was thus the most energy-efficient for heavy goods in bulk, rail travel most energy-efficient for moving humans speedily in bulk. If we are concerned with satisfying human needs with the least possible waste of energy, it remains a fact that any unit of horsepower, from whatever source of motive power is five times more efficient on rails than on a road. There are also of course, transport styles using nothing beyond human power: it is axiomatic that every town

and city should give priority to the pedestrian and the cyclist.
There are urban patterns which favour efficient public
transport and others that inhibit it. The celebrated Indian
architect-planner Charles Correa, whose task as planner (in
an honorary capacity) for New Bombay, makes our own
problems seem easily soluble, draws a telling contrast between
two cities. The layout of New Delhi, a legacy of imperialism
means that that city cannot support an economical mass
transport system. In that city, he says "it is best to be individually
mobile (whether by car or jet-propelled roller skates)". This
is why the decision-makers of India, almost all of whom travel
by private car, think that Delhi is a 'better' city than Bombay.
But Bombay is a linear city, whose growth was really
determined by the engineers of its two parallel railway lines
which give easy and cheap mobility to its teeming inhabitants.
   We can make similar comparisons nearer home. London is
a *concentric* city, whose transport problems *could* be solved by
a huge public investment in public transport, together with
'traffic calming' measures of the kind that Dutch and German
cities have pioneered, as well as by policies of 'decentralisation'.
Pandstad, Holland, by contrast, is a vast *lineal* city, and in spite
of the fact that you are all concerned with its *problems*, is a
model of how to approach the demand for personal mobility.
   But of course in Planning Design for the year 2015, we are
concerned with other aspects of urban design and planning,
besides that of transport. My friend Ian Bentley, of the Joint
Centre for Urban Design at Oxford Polytechnic, (you will
know him as co-author of the book *Responsive Environments*)
discussed only last month the "complex design situation" that
will arise from the need to integrate human and other
ecological concerns. He said:

At the cultural heart of modern industrial societies lie the values of freedom
and personal choice, which currently find practical expression through
consumerist lifestyles. Their present urban expression is ecologically
destructive, but in tackling this problem we cannot ignore the values
themselves. As designers, we must seek a balance between human desires
and their ecological effects.

He tries hard to reduce the ecological responsibilities of the
environmental designers, who might be members of any of the

particular professions represented here today, down to eight qualities. These are energy efficiency, resilience, cleanliness, wildlife support, permeability, vitality, variety and legibility.

Now these are not quite the same as the responsibilities demanded of Cornelis van Eesteren in designing for Greater Amsterdam, nor of Steen Eiler Rasmussen in designing for Greater Copenhagen, and certainly not those expected of Patrick Abercrombie in designing for Greater London. What do they imply, now or in the year 2015 for urban designers?

In terms of energy efficiency and resilience, Ian Bentley explains that two factors are important: "Minimalising the external energy needed to construct and use the place; and maximising the use of ambient – particularly solar – energy, rather than having to import it all from outside. Energy efficiency will be further boosted if buildings and urban spaces are *resilient*; able to adapt to different uses over time, rather than being wastefully torn down and rebuilt every time human aspirations change."

What do we mean by cleanliness and wildlife support? Precisely what these words suggest. Bentley suggests that "pollution, and clearance for urban redevelopment and expansion, have negative effects on many living things. Only a few aggressive and adaptable species can survive. People lose touch with (and respect for) nature, particularly since some species – rats, pigeons, cockroaches – become dangerous for humans in urban settings". He, and the rest of us, no doubt, see a need for wildlife within the city, giving space for natural predators and of the need for links into existing nearby wildlife resources, from hedgerows to reservoirs, as directly as possible. What applies to animals, birds and insects, applies of course to vegetation and trees. A policy of applying a 'wildlife grid' superimposed on the one that humans use, allows, as he puts it, "continuous 'green air' corridors from the densest built-up areas to the largest open spaces, for pollution dispersal and dust filtering".

Permeability, vitality and variety, are easy to understand. We all appreciate that "no place can offer people any sort of choice unless they can get access to and within it". Vitality implies the presence of other people, Variety means that every place has to offer a choice of experiences. His final quality, legibility, was best described by Kevin Lynch in his book *The Image of the City* which identified the key elements that people use to find their way around any place.

You and I are familiar with half a dozen vocabularies like this one, for describing the essential characteristics of intelligent, socially responsible urban design. Yet we all, visiting an unfamiliar environment, find them all absent. Professional people have been employed, money has been lavished on new developments, but an *irresponsible* environment has been created which takes no heed of the ecologically sustainable changes that we believe in. Sometimes this fact drives us to nostalgia for the compact densely populated and definable city of the past. But energy-consciousness demands dispersal. It is nearly a quarter of a century since the American anarchist and ecologist, Murray Bookchin, first expressed the energy argument for the dispersed, polynuclear city. Long before most people had the slightest interest in this issue, he observed that:

To maintain a large city requires immense quantities of coal and petroleum. By contrast, solar energy, wind power and tidal energy reach us mainly in small packets. It is hard to believe that we will ever be able to design solar collectors that can furnish us with the immense blocks of electric power produced by a giant steam plant; it is equally difficult to conceive of a battery of wind turbines that will provide us with enough electricity to illuminate Manhattan Island. If homes and factories are heavily concentrated, devices for using clean sources of energy will probably remain mere playthings; but if urban communities are reduced in size and widely spread over the land, there is no reason why these devices cannot be combined to provide us with all the amenities of an industrial civilisation. To use solar, wind and tidal power effectively, the giant city must be dispersed. A new type of community, carefully tailored to the nature and resources of a region, must replace the scrawling urban belts of today.

But who is to tailor the community to the nature and resources of a region? In practice, this is the responsibility of the planners employed by central, regional and local government. And the policies they adopt are determined, not so much by the electoral system, as by the general level of awareness of these issues in the population as a whole. This is why Geddes was right in his emphasis on the citizens rather than on the city planning officers. A book was published only a week ago in Britain called *The Dirty Man of Europe* (the author is Chris Rose and the publishers are Simon & Schuster). This book explains in detail why Britain is a major pollution exporter and in European terms, the largest producer of sulphur dioxide, and so on. How does Britain get away with it?

One of the answers that this British author gives is that of public ignorance, and if it gives you any pride, he stresses that "in the Netherlands a major public information exercise was conducted in 1985 to explain why considerable investment in acid-reducing controls on industry and power plants was needed".

But let us turn back to van Eesteren. In 1958 he remarked that:

In comparison to now, the Rhine valley used to be an Arcadia when I was young ... you could still go salmon fishing in the Rhine. But now the salmon and sturgeon have disappeared because the Rhine has been turned into a huge sewer, the sewer of Europe. The Rhine valley has been changed in a way which shocks and insults me.

I am sure that you are not satisfied with the principles of the international agreement to protect the Rhine: BATNEEC, meaning *best available technique not entailing excessive cost* so far as it affects chemical firms along that river. All the same, Germany, France, Switzerland, Luxemburg and the Netherlands have agreed on the formula of BAT, Best Available Technology, in the Rhine Action Plan. If public pressure is maintained, you professionals and your eager supporters among the citizens will achieve better.

Personally I am envious of the Netherlands for having produced a National Environmental Policy Plan, which gives dates and targets for the achievement of certain aims. I am quite sure that you are dissatisfied with it, but compare it with the British achievement of delaying any decision on anything. This is owed, not to your politicians but to the degree of public awareness of important issues. The road to an ecologically viable economy is going to be long and difficult, and I doubt if we will be there by the year 2015. The people who are professionally concerned with planning can adopt the view that it doesn't exist, or that their role is simply to say 'No' to initiatives coming from the citizens, or 'Yes' to initiatives coming from international capital. Or they can be in the forefront of the environmental educators, helping us all on the route to the transport policies, the industrial and employment policies and the habitat policies of the next century. I have already reminded you of Cornelis van Eesteren's conviction that "design is a question of ethics and morality".

There is, or if there is not, we have to discover it, an environmental ethic that could make the future human habitat 'a wonderful place to grow up in'.

References

Franziska Bollerey, 'Cornelis van Eesteren in Close-Up' in *Revista Urbanismo*,1990.

Peter Hall, *Cities of Tomorrow* (Oxford: Basil Blackwell, 1988).

Ebenezer Howard, *Garden Cities of Tomorrow* (1898) (London: Faber & Faber, 1946, 1970 *et seq.*)

Peter Kropotkin, *Fields, Factories and Workshops* (1898) (London: Freedom Press, 1985).

Patrick Geddes, *Cities in Evolution* (1915) (London: Williams & Norgate, 1949).

Ebenezer Howard, opening the discussion of a paper on 'Civics as Applied Sociology' by Patrick Geddes, read at a meeting in the London School of Economics, 18th July 1904, reprinted in Helen Mellor (editor), *The ideal City* (Leicester: University Press, 1979).

Peter Kropotkin, *Mutual Aid; A Factor in Evolution* (1902) (London: Freedom Press, 1987).

Charles Correa, *The New Landscape* (London: Butterworth, 1989).

Ian Bentley et al, *Responsive Environments* (London: Architectural Press, 1985).

Ian Bentley, 'Ecological Urban Design' in *The Architects Journal*, 24th October 1990.

Kevin Lynch, *The Image of the City* (Cambridge, Massachusetts: MIT Press, 1961).

Murray Bookchin, *Post-Scarcity Anarchism* (London: Wildwood House, 1974).

Chris Rose, *The Dirty Man of Europe* (London: Simon & Schuster, 1990).

6. Why the British don't talk about New Towns any more

All through the 1950s I worked on the drawing-board of a small private firm of architects (the practice now called Shepheard, Epstein & Hunter) on large publicly-funded projects. It was the period when that generation of British architects first explored peacetime Europe, and marvelled at the absence of rationing, which remained in Britain, not only of food, but of building materials. British architects went to Milan and were intoxicated by the sight of marble on the walls and floors of new bank building. In 1952 I slept on the floor of the Accademia in Venice and made new friends who despised marble (which they saw as a symbol of fascism) and applauded the social service architecture which they saw as a symbol of the British determination to put first things first. Even my friends, like the marine engineer Cesare Zaccaria, were full of for admiration for the British Welfare State.

Later in that year a party of Italian including Ludovico Quaroni, came to London, and it was my task to show them schemes on our drawing-boards: housing and schools for local authorities. They were full of envy for their British counterparts, not for the quality of their architecture, but for their opportunity to be useful in society. Peter Shepheard had been one of the 'backroom boys' in the wartime Ministry of Town and Country Planning (yes, we actually had one) drawing up prospective plans for the not yet designated

Lecture at the 18th International Laboratory of Architecture and Urban Design, Urbino, 3rd August 1993.

Stevenage New Town, actually named as a New Town in 1946. So I went with our visitors on the coach to that town, to see a few houses actually emerging from the usual sea of mud.

I had to explain that the state of the British economy led to the snail's pace at which the first round of New Towns got started. Quaroni and others had similar frustrated hopes in building the new village of Matera, to rehouse the cave-dwelling peasants whose misery was described in Carlo Levi's book *Christ Stopped at Eboli*. There was a public mood, both in Britain and in this country, of resolution that after the disasters of war, we should eliminate the evils of the past. I am sure that in Italy, people are reminded of this national mood whenever the films of the neo-realist period are revived on television.

In Britain, the New Towns had been put on the political agenda as a result of forty years of propaganda started by two remarkable self-educated men, Ebenezer Howard who in 1898 had produced his book *Tomorrow: A Peaceful Path to Real Reform*, republished in 1902 as *Garden Cities of Tomorrow*, and his far more politically astute disciple, Frederic Osborn. Howard, you will know, had embarked on his prototype garden cities, Letchworth and Welwyn, in 1902 and 1919, but Osborn realised that the Second World War provided the political climate to see the building of New Towns as a task of government. The New Towns Act of 1946, supported by all parties, was part of the mood of contrition, after, for example, the evacuation of city children because of bombing, had revealed the squalor of living conditions for the poor in Britain's grossly overcrowded Victorian cities. Other aspects of this resolve were the wartime plans for post-war social security, the National Health Services, and the legislation for Family Allowances or child support.

The chosen instrument for New Town building were Development Corporations, appointed by central government, and imposed upon the normal structure of local authorities, sometimes with, and sometimes contrary to their wishes. The Development Corporations were to have a limited life; they were given the task of providing the urban infrastructure, building houses and recreational facilities, attracting industry, and if necessary building factories, and encouraging what was known as social development. Other existing authorities were responsible for schools and health services.

Of the 32 New Towns designated between 1946 and 1970 (none have been designated since then) all the Development Corporations have been closed apart from those in Scotland which have been given a few more years of life. For the people who live in them the New Towns are, of course, not new at all. The pioneer settlers are grandparents, and for two generations of children they are the same boring old town as anyone else's home town. The British New Towns have attracted great interest and envy in many countries, in totalitarian dictatorships as much as in democracies. But, as my title notes, the British don't talk about New Towns any more. It would be more accurate to say that they talk about them in tones of bored denigration.

Since, by comparison with the attempts over the same period at the regeneration of old cities or the suburban extensions of existing cities in Britain, the New Towns have been an economic, financial and social success, this is an interesting fact, very significant for us architects or town-planners, or as citizens. For it illustrates a profound change in the climate. Let me demonstrate this.

In 1946, Lord Reith (the famous founder of the BBC) who was the chairman of the committee appointed to advise the government on New Towns, declared that they would be "an essay in civilisation". Twenty years later, Leslie Lane, director of the thoroughly establishment amenity body, the Civic Trust saw the New Towns as "the greatest conscious programme of city building ever undertaken by any country in history". But last year, on 24th January 1992, the 25th anniversary of Milton Keynes and the date of the demise of its development corporation, were celebrated in a leading article in *The Times*, under the title 'Paradise Mislaid'. For *The Times* the occasion was "a memorial to a tradition of social engineering that must be seen as dead and buried. Hardly, however, to be mourned". It found that "an eagerness to force large numbers of people out of city centres, shared with authoritarians in less democratic societies, led to the desertion and dereliction of many of Britain's inner cities and the spoliation of millions of acres of countryside," and that "residents, many moved compulsorily and callously, found themselves in single-class towns with poor services and a lack of communal continuity vital to a humane neighbourhood". For the leader-writer, "Milton Keynes was the last desperate throw of a generation of British planners who were distasteful of the traditional British town and cities and had the political power and public money to fashion the environment to their will ... The architect was god and history was the devil". And, of course, "from Crawley and Corby to Skelmersdale, Washington and Cumbernauld, new-town blues became a widespread syndrome".

The climate has indeed changed, and you will notice that the architect is now cast in the role of villain. The comments in *The Times* are fascinating as a symptom of the rewriting of history needed for the moral climate of Britain in the 1990s. As reporting of facts, not a word of these comments are true.

Nobody was "moved compulsorily and callously" to the New Towns. The callousness and compulsion happened in the old cities in the mania for demolition and rehousing in tower blocks of the 1950s and '60s. Residents choose to move to New Towns for very normal reasons, for the prospect of better housing, better employment opportunities, better access to the countryside, and above all, better futures for their children. The New Towns were not the cause of the problems of the old cities, they were a positive response to it. David Hall of the Town and Country Planning Association was quick to point out in connection with those despoiled millions of acres that "the total development area of the 28 new towns of Great Britain is 255,487 acres (0.45% of the total land area) and contains only 7.5% of all the new housing built in Britain since 1951" and that of outward movement of population from London only about 7% of the people moved to the new or expanded towns. Nor have medical statisticians found any evidence for the particular form of neurosis described as 'new-town blues'. People can be happy or miserable anywhere.

I imagine that we have moved a long way from the propaganda of the Modern Movement that suggested that people would be happy as a result of architecture and planning. The most we can claim for a decent physical environment is that it has often eliminated some of the more avoidable kinds of misery. But the most obvious source of misery is in fact the absence of an income or of purchasing power, and the most obvious source of an income is a job. In the days when the New Towns were conceived, it was automatically assumed by politicians and by the public that full employment was the first aim of government policy. The New Towns had a truly remarkable record in attracting new industry (not in luring old industry, as is sometimes implied, from old centre of employment). They have also been buffeted, like anywhere else, by the sudden closure of industries that hit Corby and Skelmersdale, or through the happy ending of the Cold War, that has brought employment disasters to places like Stevenage or Hatfield. Remember that Milton Keynes, with none of the financial inducements of assisted parts of the country, attracted 83,000 new jobs. And while it may shock moralists like me, plenty of people from that city assured me that the ultimate factors in the decision by the directors of a multi-national company to locate in Milton Keynes were *not* the ones which would have been uppermost to an economist, but the ones which would occur to an estate agent: the presence of high-quality 'executive' houses, easy access to an international airport, luxury hotels, private schools and golf courses, the green landscape and parks.

But what about the overwhelming majority of New Town populations? It did not occur to us at the time, as we didn't assume that government policy would shift to the redistribution of income from the poor to the rich, but we can now see that a very important New Town function was that it enabled low-income, house-renting families to join the outward movement from the overcrowded Victorian city, that has been a demographic feature of the twentieth century, taken absolutely for granted by the affluent. This escape route has now been completely closed for people who can't afford to buy a house. What this means is that the New Towns have ceased to cater for any new incoming members of the low-wage-earning, rent-paying slice of the community. Admirers in other countries of the British New Town achievement must look elsewhere for the social policy they once admired. This explains why there are homeless young couples in Crawley or Harlow, or Milton Keynes, just as there are everywhere else.

But let me turn to the architectural aspects, and the assumption that in New Town building, "the architect was God". The first major criticism of New Town architecture came from within the architectural world. In 1953 an issue of the *Architectural Review* on the 'Failure of the New Towns' criticised the 'prairie planning' of streets, of low-rise, low-density housing, inhabited by, so the journal said, "footsore housewives and cycle-weary workers", indistinguishable from any suburban estate anywhere, so that, it was claimed, "what should have been a great adventure has come to nothing".

Defenders of the New Towns were quick to point to errors in the critics' assumptions and confusions about residential densities, and land economists made careful surveys to show that "there are no low-density new towns". They proved that the New Town approach was far less of an encroachment on the national stock of agricultural land, than the suburban expansion of the 1930s, or that of the post-war years.

But behind the polemics about densities is a big architectural issue. We all like old towns and villages with the continuous street facade and its comfortable sense of enclosure. It was not the perversity of architects that made it impossible in new residential areas to have the same quality, but the fact that the environment in Britain is over-regulated by every kind of authority. The absurdly wide roads and pavements with scarcely any traffic, the extravagant provision of turning circles for the biggest conceivable vehicles were there because of the demands for easy access for the largest of possible fire appliances, furniture, removal vans or refuse collection trucks. Layouts had to meet the maximum standards of the highway engineer, not the aspirations of architects.

As for the opinions of residents: the most-loved and the least-lovely housing I have ever visited in a New Town were at Runcorn. The least-loved was designed by a world-famous architect, Jim Stirling, the most-loved was by the anonymous architectural staff of the Runcorn Development Corporation. There is a rather similar story from Milton Keynes. A very sensitive architect and environmental psychologist, Jeff Bishop, from the School for Advanced Urban Studies at Bristol, led a team to study what the people who lived there thought and felt about Milton Keynes. He explained that "the corporation became the home for a group of young architects ... known in Milton Keynes as 'the undertakers' because of their penchant for black suits ... For them, this new town was the classic sheet of blank paper ... They won out to the extent that each was 'given' a grid-square to design and they did just that – starting from scratch as if nothing else would ever exist."

Milton Keynes Development Corporation also employed the most currently-respected prestige-laden architects as consultants: Norman Foster, Richard MacCormac, Archigram and Edward Cullinan, among many. But Jeff Bishop's team found that the work of the most famous architects at Milton Keynes was, with one significant exception, liked least, while the houses, whether publicly or privately-built, that most resemble our traditional picture of house and home, were liked most. The exception, in the work of famous architects was Eaglestone, designed, I am happy to say, by Ralph Erskine.

Bishop also found that "at the outset the research team were told that people find Milton Keynes confusing and they get lost. This was patently not true of the residents, so what was the source of this rumour? A chance encounter provided the answer: that those who get lost seem to be predominantly visiting architects and planners who come with a pre-conceived idea of' what clues and landmarks a 'city' should offer ... and are then confused when such clues are not apparent ... The residents of course have no such problems."

He concluded that "Milton Keynes is a success – to the extent that one might add *despite* the planners. Residents see themselves not as living in the new city of Milton Keynes, but in Linford or Heelands, etc., which they see as a series of villages. They conceive of Milton Keynes as "somewhere only a little better than usual, a normal landscape dotted with villages which have somehow managed to appear without the countryside, complete with by-passes". Shrewdly he notes the way professional ideologies contain a set of perceptions of what is urban and what is rural, and these are *threatened* by suburban and garden city environments precisely because they are "symbols of individual aspirations rather than corporate ones".

You might very well conclude that if there had been a habit of participation or simply consultation with the citizens many of the mistakes of the professionals in the New Towns might have been avoided. But in looking at the British New Town story and why we don't talk about it any more, the overwhelming impression is of change in the psychology of the British. When the New Towns were conceived, we were a nation of *neophiliacs*, looking forward hopefully to the new. Today we are a nation of *antiquarians*, in love with everything old, and with a highly selective, often fictional, past. The older the house you live in, the higher your social status.

Naturally our mood of antiquarianism affects our attitude to buildings and places. And of course it affects the architecture that is commissioned today, and explains the vogue for neo-classical and neo-vernacular architecture. And it is linked with the phenomenon which Giancarlo on his visit to London in June this year described as "the indecent triumph of the market-led economy". We don't talk about our New Towns any more because we are *ashamed* of the naive social-service ideal in architecture and planning that inspired them. The official historian of Milton Keynes, Terence Bendixson, remarks that "turning the warm-hearted, motherly, public-service-oriented Milton Keynes of the 1970s into a slim-jim, self-financing, property investment machine designed to suit the commercial disciplines of the 1980s was a huge task". But the sad fact is that in fact it was the easiest task in the world in a country like Britain which, since the dethronement of the regimes in Albania and Romania is the most centralised nation in Europe.

You may have the impression that I am a defender of the British New Towns. But I am in fact a severe critic on grounds which never occur to their fashionable detractors. The pattern of a Development Corporation, appointed by government, was modelled, back in 1946 on John Reith's experience of the British Broadcasting Corporation of which he was the famous Director and on that of the Labour politician Herbert Morrison, of the London Passenger Transport Board which he founded, long before the Second World War. One sad thing is that the pattern never evolved. Built into it was conflict with the elected local authorities. Some of the development corporations went to great length to become friends and allies of the local councils. Others did not. There has been a failure of social or organisational imagination in not devising a more popular mechanism. I myself, as an anarchist have for years advocated a 'Do-it-yourself New Town'. Some place, somewhere in Britain where the regulations can be abandoned, and where people are invited to make their own New Town, just to see what we can learn from the results. There are, after all, important lessons from the experience of the *barrios* and *barriadas* of Latin America.

But the saddest thing about British New Town history has been the abandonment of the central point of Ebenezer Howard's Garden City proposals of almost a century ago. He believed that the Garden City should belong to its citizens in perpetuity. Once the money borrowed for its development had been paid back, the income arising from the increased value of the land itself would flow back to the community whose presence had created the 'unearned increment' of property values. As the geographer Peter Hall explains, the legislation that set up the New Towns in 1946 implied that this increasing income should be appropriated by the Government. This "destroyed the essence of Howard's plan, which was to fund the creation of self-governing local welfare states. Top-down planning triumphed over bottom-up. Britain would have the shell of Howard's Garden City vision without the substance."

A later government in 1959 set up a Commission for the New Towns which was to take over the assets when the Development Corporations come to an end. This Commission was to "have regard to the purpose for which the town was developed and to the convenience and welfare of persons residing, working or carrying on business there". But governments being what they are, this Commission had to follow the Thatcher government's policy of selling publicly owned assets. Its own publicity explains that:

Since 1979 the Government has been undertaking one of the most important aspects of its 'privatisation' policy without the glare of publicity associated with British Telecom, British Gas or Water Authority flotations – the sale of new town assets ... The principal responsibility of the Commission now is to realise the taxpayers' investment in its towns and achieve 'normalisation' as soon as practicable."

So the New Towns are being normalised, and have become exactly like anywhere else. If you were blindfolded and dropped by parachute into any housing, shopping, educational or recreational or working environment in Britain, apart from your attempts to identify the architecture as that of the '50s, '60s, or '70s, how would you know whether you were in a New Town or in the suburban expansion or rebuilding of existing towns? Would the people around you, or the houses, shops, schools or factories be any different? Would the grass be any greener or the buses any more frequent? Normalisation has won, and whatever the hopes of their pioneers, the New Towns are just like anywhere else. Some of us had hopes that they might be just a little better. Perhaps that is another reason why the British don't talk about their New Towns any more.

References

Ebenezer Howard, *Garden Cities of Tomorrow* (1902) (New edition, Attic Books 1989).

Jeff Bishop, *Milton Keynes, The Best of Both Worlds. Public and Professional Views of a New City* (School for Advanced Urban Studies Occasional Paper 24, 1986).

Colin Ward, *Talking Houses* (Freedom Press, 1990).

Colin Ward, *New Town, Home Town: The Lessons of Experience* (Gulbenkian Foundation, 1993).

7. Unexpected pioneers of town and country planning in Britain

I was gratified when Riccardo Mariani and Léopold Veuve asked me to talk about some of the key figures in the evolution of town and country planning in Britain. I was not the obvious choice as I am neither an academic nor a planner, although I worked in architecture and planning for many years. I am a writer, and my books tend to be about housing, and often about popular and unofficial uses of the environment: for example the relationship between children and their environment in city and country, the history of unofficial settlements – shanty towns or *bicoques*, allotment gardens or *jardins potager*, or *orti urbani*, *huertos comunalos* or *schrebergärten*.

I am interested in *bricolage*, in the interstices of the official system in which people do their own thing. You might conclude that mine is an anarchist approach to planning, and you would be right. However, my task is to trace the stream of ideas about planning in Britain through its most significant advocates, and if there is one book I should urge you to read it is not a book of mine, but a book by Britain's foremost urban geographer, Peter Hall, who is professor of planning at the Bartlett School of Architecture, University College, London, and is also Director of the Institute of Urban and Regional Development at Berkeley, California. His book, published in 1988, is *Cities of Tomorrow: An Intellectual History of Urban Planning and Design in the Twentieth Century*. As early as page 3 of his book,

Lecture at the post-graduate course on Urbanism, Geneva University, and Lausanne Polytechnic, 27th September 1993.

Professor Hall vindicates my own approach. Under the heading
'The Anarchist Roots of the Planning Movement', he explains:

Specifically, the book will argue that in the process of belatedly translating
ideal into reality, there occurred a rather monstrous perversion of history.
The really striking point is that many, though by no means all, of the early
visions of the planning movement stemmed from the anarchist movement
which flourished in the last decades of the nineteenth century and the first
years of the twentieth. That is true of Howard, of Geddes and of the
Regional Planning Association of America, as well as of many derivatives
on the mainland of Europe. (To be sure, it was very definitely untrue of Le
Corbusier, who was an authoritarian centralist, and of most members of the
City Beautiful movement, who were faithful servants of finance capitalism
or totalitarian dictators.) The vision of these anarchist pioneers was not
merely of an alternative built form, but of an alternative society, neither
capitalist nor bureaucratic-socialistic: a society based on voluntary
co-operation among men and women, working and living in small,
self-governing commonwealths.

Professor Hall goes on to say that, "When however the time
at last came for their ideals to be translated into bricks and
mortar, the irony was that – more often than not – this
happened through the agency of state bureaucracies, which
they would have hated. How this came about, how far it was
responsible for the subsequent disillusionment with the idea
of planning, will be a central question that the book must
address". And elsewhere in his book (pages 142-145) he traces
back the regionalist ideology of twentieth century planning to
four nineteenth century anarchists, two French and two
Russian: Pierre-Joseph Proudhon, Michael Bakunin, Elisée
Reclus and Peter Kropotkin.

My purpose today is to talk about the planners, not about
the anarchists, but since we are in the Swiss Confederation, I
must stress that Proudhon, in advocating regionalism and
federalism, took as a model the Swiss supremacy of the
commune as the unit of social organisation, linked by the
canton, with a purely administrative *federal council*; that
Bakunin, talking at the meeting in Geneva of the League for
Peace and Freedom on 9th September 1897, advocated a
United States of Europe based on what he called "the free
federation of individuals into communes, communes into
provinces, provinces into nations", and spoke admiringly of
the Swiss Confederation, "practising federation so successfully

today" as he put it. The irony was that he was being carefully reported on by the Swiss police, as was the geographer Elisée Reclus, a refugee from the Paris Commune, working on his *Nouvelle Géographie Universelle*, and lecturing on geography, also in Geneva. Another geographer and revolutionary, Peter Kropotkin came to Switzerland in 1872. He was urged to visit Sonvilier in a valley of the Jura Hills, where the watch-case makers in their home workshops had linked with the workers of the Neuchâtel area to form the Jura Federation of the International Workingmen's Association. He was converted to anarchist ideas by this encounter with this nest of precision industry combined with food production. After his imprisonment in Russia, and his escape to Britain, he returned. His wife Sofia earned a BSc at the University of Geneva, but his defence of the assassins of Tsar Alexander II was too much for the Swiss Federal Council, and they were expelled from this country. One of the significant books he wrote back in Britain was *Fields, Factories and Workshops*, arguing the viability of a localised small-workshop economy, an integrated education and the combination of brain-work and manual work.

To the influences of these European anarchists on the founding fathers of the planning movement in Britain, we have to add that of the celebrated English craftsman and socialist, William Morris. His reputation survives, almost a century after his death, because he addressed all those issues which actually affect the quality of the daily lives of men, women and children. Morris is often dismissed as a romantic medievalist who ignored the machine age. But a famous essay of his, *A Factory as it Might Be*, written in 1884 and certainly read by our four planning pioneers, Morris remarked "machines of the most ingenious and best-approved kinds will be used when necessary, but will be used simply to save human labour". In other words he wanted the *appropriate* use of machinery. Having established the range of influences on them, I can now introduce the four pioneers.

The first was Patrick Geddes, a Scottish biologist, and a close friend of the Reclus brothers, Elie and Elisée. They introduced him to the thought of the French sociologist Frédéric Le Play, and the trilogy of Folk, Work and Place as the key to the understanding of human civilisation and the culture of cities. Deeply influenced by Reclus, he evolved the idea of the 'Valley Section' as the key to understanding human activities in their physical milieu, from the mountain through the country to the city and its port. It was Geddes who coined the slogan 'Survey Before Plan' and who invented the word *conurbation* to describe the way in which electric power, and the internal combustion engine were agents for both the dispersal and the conglomeration of cities.

He was also famous for initiating the renewal of the ancient slum tenements of Edinburgh, for starting the world's first self-governing student hostel, and for the Outlook Tower at the heart that city, with a *camera obscura* at its top, intended as a laboratory for the citizens to understand their city and to plan for its renewal. Geddes has a deeply disturbing effect on the people he met. He was one of those people who take hold of you in the street, talking endlessly and waving his arms around: an erratic, disorganised and overbearing genius who anticipated every one of our late-twentieth century preoccupations, from the energy crisis to women's liberation. He was always looking for the right disciple to carry his message onwards. The best one that he actually found was the American writer Lewis Mumford, whose books on the evolution of technology and of urban settlements are full of his influence and of that of Kropotkin.

To give you something of the flavour of his approach to the activities of the professional planner, I must quote a paragraph from one of the reports he prepared during the First World War for the rulers of Indian cities. Reporting on the towns in the Madras Presidency in 1915, Geddes remarked:

Town-planning is not mere place-planning, nor even work-planning. If it is to be successful it must be folk-planning. This means that its task is to find the right places for each sort of people; places where they will really flourish. To give people, in fact, the care that we give when transplanting flowers, instead of harsh evictions and arbitrary instructions to 'move on', delivered in the manner of officious amateur policemen.

The second of these pioneers was, of course, Ebenezer Howard, a stenographer or shorthand-writer who had listened to the debates among more important people about the appalling problems of the Victorian cities. British cities in his day had a horrifyingly overcrowded population while rural areas were sunk in depression because Free Trade allowed cheap agricultural imports from America and the British Empire, and were experiencing a continual drain of population.

Howard read and listened, absorbed the ideas of utopian thinkers, and those of both Geddes and Kropotkin, and produced his solution as an amalgam designed with singular skill to attract the widest possible support.

He borrowed £50 to subsidise the publisher and in 1898 produced his book *Tomorrow: a Peaceful Path to Real Reform*, full of home-made diagrams advocating the Garden City idea. In the following year a group of enthusiasts founded the Garden Cities Association, which is now the Town and Country Planning Association, and in 1902 his book reappeared under the title *Garden Cities of Tomorrow*. This obscure inventor's book, even though its message was endlessly diluted and misunderstood, became the most influential document of the whole twentieth century. Seventy years after it appeared, the chairman of Milton Keynes Development Corporation, (a socialist industrialist, Lord Campbell of Eskan) remarked how astonishingly fresh and relevant were the principles derived from Howard, stressing that "Howard wanted dispersal in order to make possible the humane redevelopment of the inner city".

Campbell summarised Howard's essential vocabulary as:
a) Small scale settlements
b) A basically co-operative economy
c) A marriage of town and country
d) Control by the community of its own development
e) Control by the community of the land values it creates
f) The importance of a social environment in which the individual could develop his own ideas and manage his own affairs in co-operation with his neighbours
g) The strength of the family unit in the community.

Howard believed in co-operative, rather than state initiative, and in 1902 his supporters formed the Garden City Pioneer Company to gather the funds to develop the First Garden City at Letchworth, believing that a practical example was more persuasive than theory. There he gathered his most influential disciple, Frederic Osborn, and they embarked in the aftermath of the First World War on the development of Welwyn Garden City, also in Hertfordshire, north of London. Osborn was to play a vital part in the propaganda that persuaded the British government to embark on its New Towns programme after the Second World War, and I will have something more to say about this.

But among the links between Geddes and Howard, I should mention an occasion in the year 1904, when Patrick Geddes delivered a paper on 'Civics as Applied Sociology'. Howard was asked to open the discussion of the paper from Geddes. He remarked that:

... while the age we live in is the age of the great closely completed, overcrowded city, there are already signs, for those who can read them, of a coming change so great and so momentous that the twentieth century will be known as the period of the great exodus.

This was a very prophetic observation, and the question for everyone concerned with city planning all through the twentieth century has been whether this exodus from the cities should be absorbed in endless suburbs, or in the leap over green belts to towns and villages in the rural environment, made accessible by universal personal transport, or whether planned provision should be made for it. To introduce this issue, I have to turn to the third of the pioneers, Raymond Unwin.

Unwin was a young man from industrial Yorkshire, apprenticed as an engineer for a coal-mining company, for whom he was employed on building pithead baths and miners' cottages. He became deeply involved in the socialist propaganda of William Morris and Edward Carpenter, joining his wife's brother Barry Parker in an architectural partnership. In 1901 they became the designers for the new village called New Earswick, near York, for the Rowntree Chocolate company, and in 1903 they won the competition for the planning of Ebenezer Howard's First Garden City at Letchworth. Soon afterwards they were invited to plan the Hampstead Garden Suburb in North London.

Meanwhile the propaganda of Patrick Geddes and Ebenezer Howard was beginning to affect government attitudes. The reforming Liberal government of the first decade of this century, which initiated health and unemployment insurance as well as old age pensions, introduced the first British legislation, the Housing and Town Planning Act of 1909. This was 'enabling' law-making which could be acted upon or ignored, like all the planning laws of the next thirty years, but it was seized upon by Howard, Geddes and Unwin as a legitimation of their propaganda.

Raymond Unwin seized the opportunity to produce a 400-page book, full of the wisdom he had been accumulating over the past decade, as much on housing design as urban design, drawing upon the propaganda of Geddes and Howard, upon American experience and on the design precepts of Camillo Sitte's *Der Städtebau*, or *L'art de bâtir les Villes*. In 1914, Unwin became a public servant, as Chief Town Planning Inspector to the Local Government Board, deciding to exercise his influence from inside the governmental apparatus. He was the prime influence behind the Tudor Walters Committee of 1918 which established standards of accommodation and layout for publicly-funded housing between the two world wars. In 1911 he had observed the Parkway Plan that established a green 'cordon sanitaire' around Chicago, and he influenced the 'Lex Adenauer' after the First World War, which established a 'Green Girdle' round Cologne.

Raymond Unwin tried hard to find an opportunity, within the machinery of government, to influence policy on planning, and in 1927 was appointed as Technical Adviser to the Greater London Regional Planning Committee, which had been set up by Neville Chamberlain as Minister of Health in 1927. This body was funded on a pathetically small basis by central and local government and issued two reports. The second report of 1933 was published when the money had run out, and Unwin subsidised it from his own income. He advocated a 'Green Girdle' around London and recommended the development of a series of new towns around the metropolis to absorb the inevitable outward movement of population and industry. But both central and local government had lost interest, and only the Garden Cities Association took notice of his report.

The last hero of the story was Patrick Abercrombie. He too was an architect, but very early in his career he was enthralled by the propaganda for civic survey and regional planning of Patrick Geddes. When a research fellowship in town planning and civic design was endowed at the University of Liverpool he was the first holder, just as he was the first editor of the *Town Planning Review*, and followed this with a succession of academic posts in Liverpool and London. In the period between the two world wars he produced a long series of planning reports on British regions following the precepts of Geddes. Writing about his contribution, a colleague, William Holford, wrote:

Abercrombie was the link between the enlightened amateur of the nineteenth century and the professional expert of the twentieth. Looking through some thirty pre-war reports, all delightfully presented but now largely superseded and dust-laden, one is made aware of Abercrombie's immense industry and fertility; but also of the fact that although they were persuasive, and beginning to be influential, they were not yet backed by administrative power or by economic incentives.

It was the Second World War that gave Abercrombie his opportunity and his popular fame. Wartime, and the national resolve to eliminate the social evils of pre-war Britain – chronic unemployment and desperate overcrowding of population in the cities – made it necessary for the government to promise that something better would follow after the war. Abercrombie rose to the occasion. Firstly he prepared the County of London Plan of 1943 for the London County Council, and while working on it was busily engaged on producing his Greater London Plan of 1944, published by the central government in the following year. In it he argued for planned dispersal to New Towns beyond a Green Belt, following Unwin's earlier recommendations, and it is worth noting his 'Personal Foreword' to his Plan. He wrote:

The Plan thus prepared, with this multifarious guidance and collaboration, is now completed, so far as it is possible to say that the stage of finality can be reached by a living organism. There is now a chance and a similar one may not occur again of getting the main features of this programme of redistributed population and work carried through rapidly and effectively, thereby reducing overcrowding and locating industry in conjunction. The difficulties in normal times of moving people and industry are rightly stressed; but people and industry will go where accommodation is made available. Moreover, the war has made migration a familiar habit. Give a man and his wife a first-rate house, a community, and occupation of various kinds reasonably near at hand, with a regional framework which enables them to move freely and safely about, to see their friends and enjoy the advantages of London; add to these a wide freedom of choice, and they will not grumble in the years immediately following the war. The industrialist, if he is asked whether he is prepared to submit to the guidance of a government official, will probably protest. But if he is offered a choice of sites, with every modern facility (including labour) provided, and in addition a licence to build and access to building materials and labour, he will jump at the chance to get started as quickly as possible. Moreover, if Trading Estates are laid out ready for hire and actually a certain amount of building is done for small enterprises, these sites and factories will be eagerly taken up: always, of course, provided they are sited in the most suitable positions .... Courage is needed to seize the moment when it arrives and to make a resolute start.

Abercrombie went on, with various collaborators, to produce many further planning reports, for Hull, Weymouth, Edinburgh, the Clyde valley and the West Midlands, as well for many city regions in other countries. But it is for the Greater London Plan that he is most remembered. Some observers see the Greater London Plan as the 'high-water mark' of prescriptive planning on a grand scale. Thus Professor Gordon Cherry in his book on *The Evolution of British Town Planning* (1974) notes how Abercrombie:

... in one package of proposals, outlined what needed to be done. The issues had been narrowed down to black and white alternatives, and in a master sweep he sketched the solutions as one integrated physical and social design for the metropolis and its region. Today this would be unthinkable. The Greater London Development Plan of 1969 was quite a different planning exercise, finding the issues not clear cut but wide open for various interpretations; no finite solutions could be postulated. The difference over just a quarter of a century sums up all that has happened by way of change in planning. It is argued, therefore, that town planning is really a question of policy planning; it is an on-going, problem-oriented activity, with no fixed end products, but with objectives set by perceived social goals, changing over time. A new task of planning cities is being recognised, where complexity and uncertainty are the keynotes:

Now I agree, temperamentally, with Professor Cherry, but I

have to report that the Greater London Development Plan of
1969, prepared at enormous public expense, had a minimal
effect and has by now been written out of history, while
Abercrombie's 1944 plan, and by implication, Unwin's 1933
proposals, stay in the history of what actually happened,
simply because they resulted in recognisable policies which
spread to other British cities.

The first was that of the Green Belt. Unlike many planning
policies, this is actually popular with citizens. Green Belts are
seen by the citizen as a Good Thing. They have had
unexpected results, like the escalation of property values
within them and in country towns beyond the fringe, and that
can be seen as another mechanism to prevent the urban poor
from joining the predicted exodus from the overcrowded city.
Peter Hall and his colleagues in their magisterial study of *The
Containment of Urban England*, quoted a government minister
who said long ago that Green Belts may not be at all useful or
beautiful, and may indeed not be very green, "but without
them the town would never end; the very essence of the green
belt is that it is a *stopper*".

The second result of the propaganda of Geddes and Howard,
reinforced by the official recommendations from Unwin and
Abercrombie is the New Towns policy embarked upon by
post-war British Governments. As a policy it is now over. The
last of the New Town Development Corporations in England
and Wales closed down last year, and those in Scotland will
close before the end of this decade. I myself was commissioned
to write a book on the lessons to be learned from the New
Towns, in a book published this year called *New Town, Home
Town: the lessons of experience*.

Naturally I have many criticisms of the policy, but in
evaluating the New Towns the first thing to be said is that by
contrast to all other programmes for coping with the problems
of the cities, the New Towns have been a financial success,
and that they were one of the only routes out of the
overcrowded city available to families with low incomes. In
terms of Ebenezer Howard's hopes, simply as a result of
government policy, they have not succeeded. He wanted the
income resulting from the enhanced values that the presence

of new settlements was bound to accumulate to become the collective property of the citizens themselves. The New Town would belong to its inhabitants. But of course it does not. The present British Government has been selling off the assets of the New Towns as rapidly as it can. So I have to conclude by agreeing with Peter Hall's Diagnosis that the New Town legislation "destroyed the essence of Howard's plan, which was to fund the creation of self-governing welfare states. Top-down planning triumphed over bottom-up. Britain would have the shell of Howard's Garden City vision without the substance".

I began by reminding you of Professor Hall's view that the twentieth century planning movement in Britain began with the ideology of nineteenth century anarchists. I an sorry to say that the evolution of our technical capacity has not been accompanied by a comparable social evolution. We had a period when it was assumed that governmental initiatives would solve all problems, and we are now in a period when it is assumed that public expenditure is wicked and unproductive, while private investment for private profit will solve all problems. By now we are all sophisticated enough to know that both attitudes are too simple to be true. The hopes of the pioneers of planning for popular initiatives in re-shaping our environment have not been fulfilled. We cannot blame the planning, pioneers for this. They did what they could.

But these four pioneers do illustrate the dilemmas that face us all, whether we are concerned with town and country planning as professional experts or as citizens. Ebenezer Howard was an amateur inventor who, as Professor Hall correctly says, was more interested in social processes than in physical planning. He attracted a team of practical people, like Frederic Osborn or C.B. Purdom, who tried to fit his ideas into the ordinary machinery of politics and policy. The same is true of Patrick Geddes, throwing out ideas about a participatory democracy, and searching for interpreters to give these ideas a physical reality. Raymond Unwin, a master of domestic architecture and a faithful follower of William Morris and the Arts and Crafts movement, joined the administrative machinery of government to fight from within the official system, and finally, Patrick Abercrombie, another architect, spent twenty years as Professor of Civic Design at Liverpool and another ten as Professor of Town Planning at University College in London, and was employed by many of the towns and regions of Britain to produce surveys and reports intended as a guide for their future.

Did they make the right choices? Have we benefited, at the end of the twentieth century from the decisions they made and the policies they recommended? These are some of the questions we might want to discuss together.

8. Self-help and sustainability: the coming dilemmas of planning

It is fifty years since George Orwell wrote his series of essays on the politics of the English language, which he was to epitomise in an appendix to his novel *Nineteen Eighty-Four* in the concepts of *Newspeak* and *Doublespeak*, and, of course, *Prolefeed*. Now I have the impression that the pace of distortion and degeneration of the meanings we give to words and phrases has become more rapid since Orwell's day.

Consider what has happened to the concept of participation since Skeffington's report on *People and Planning* in 1969. Or consider the more rapid decline into fatuity of the word heritage over a much shorter period, so that you and I, when we use it, feel obliged to distance ourselves from it by putting it into quotation marks. Or consider the sinister uses made by government and business-school graduates of worthy aspirations like enabling and empowerment. For me, the most chilling moment in Molly Dinecti's brilliant series of BBC2 films on the financial crisis of the London Zoo came when she was interviewing one of the directors. He was full of managementspeak and explained the necessity for empower-ment of the Zoo's workforce. "Once you've given them empowerment", he said, "you've got them in the grinder".

The Frederic Osborn Memorial Lecture to the Royal Society of Arts, London, 2nd March 1994.

I have to warn you that the concept of sustainability is subject
to the same process. It was put into our vocabulary by the
Brundtland Commission's report in 1987, and has taken over
from a series of other attempts to define the same notion, like
"the steady-state economy", which have been current since
people began to take our environmental dilemmas seriously
in the late 1960s and early 1970s. Brundtland defined the idea
of sustainable development as "development which meets
present needs without compromising the ability of future
generations to achieve their needs and aspirations" (*Our
Common Future*, World Commission on Environment and
Development, OUP, 1987).

The ablest account of the implications of this for those
concerned with environmental policies and aspirations comes
very appropriately from the Town and Country Planning
Association, the voluntary body with which Frederic Osborn
was intimately involved for over sixty years. It convened a
group of specialists to spend three years in preparing the report
Planning for a Sustainable Environment (Earthscan, 1993). And
the book's editor, Professor Andrew Blowers, in the opening
page, puts our situation in a world context, stressing that "the
richest countries of the Organisation for Economic
Co-operation and Development (OECD) – with only 6% of
the world's population – consume about eleven times more
energy per head and create half the carbon dioxide from fossil
fuels, three-quarters of the industrial and four-fifths of the
hazardous wastes".

In other words it is the rich who should change their habits
before imposing even greater deprivations on the poor. This,
of course, is the opposite of what happens in the real world.
We can all cite examples of the deliberate export of hazardous
waste from the rich, consuming countries to poor countries
which usually have less stringent and less enforceable
standards of control of dangerous processes and dangerous
materials.

But wealth and poverty co-exist in both rich and poor
countries. Dr Janice Perlman, from the Mega-cities Project of
New York University, stresses that "every first-world city has
within it a third-world city of malnutrition, infant mortality,

homelessness and unemployment. And conversely, every third-world city has within it a first-world city of high tech, high fashion and high finance". You and I can watch the increase in this contrast in the cities of both poor and rich worlds. For Britain I rely on the testimony of a former Conservative cabinet minister, Ian Gilmour, for the evidence that "relative poverty grew significantly during the 1980s, encompassing nearly one-tenth of the population in 1979 and nearly one-fifth in 1987. Even more disturbing, children fared worse than society as a whole during this period, the proportion living in poverty doubling to reach 26% in 1987". He goes on to relate the growth of impoverishment to the enrichment of the rich:

In the 1980s, for the first time for fifty years and, possibly, for more than a century, the poorer half of the population saw its share of total national income shrink. In 1979 the poorest fifth of the population had just under 10% of post-tax income and the richest fifth had 37%. By 1989 the share of the poorest fifth had fallen to 7%, while the share of the richest fifth had risen to 43%. The rich got richer and the poor got poorer. (Ian Gilmour, *Dancing with Dogma*, Simon & Schuster, 1992)

We can't brush aside his figures. They are confirmed in the latest publication from the Central Statistical Office, *Social Trends 1994* (HMSO, 1994). Information of this kind is bound to affect our attitude to the measures taken by governments to approach the goal of sustainability. Professor David Pearce addressed the Society on 20th March 1991 ('A Sustainable World: who cares, who pays?' in *RSA Journal*, July 1991), and argued that:

We are not, for example, going to achieve internationally agreed targets for reducing global warming unless we tax greenhouse gases, and especially carbon dioxide. That means taxing coal, oil and gas, with the highest tax being on coal, the lowest on gas, since that is the ranking of their carbon content. If we adopt such 'carbon taxes' then we have once again made the polluter pay. But, however we make the initial polluter pay, they will pass some, not all, of the regulatory cost on to the consumer. That is exactly what the polluter pays principle requires. We, the consumer, must also pay. If we do not, we shall not send the right signals back to the producer of the polluting product. The higher the price the less we will buy – that is a piece of market information for the producer. It tells him or her to change technology – to become green.

If we translate this point of view into the real world we find
the Chancellor seizing upon the chance to raise revenue by
flat rate taxes on domestic fuel users, with a token increase in
state pensions, and attempting to silence criticism with the
claim that the measure is "Britain's strategy for meeting our
Rio commitments to restrain carbon dioxide emissions". I
think there are two things to be said about this and about
Professor Pearce's stipulations. The first is that the domestic
consumer of electricity has no means of knowing whether his
or her source is derived from burning coal, oil, gas or rubbish,
or of the type of filter on emissions, or whether it derives from
hydro-electricity, or indeed, whether it derives from nuclear
power, or the new and welcome burgeoning of windfarms.
The consumer is unable to send the right signals back to the
producer.

The second point relates to our government's preference for
regressive as opposed to progressive taxation. Patricia O'Donnell
pointed out last year that "The poor spend nearly 10% of
disposable income on heating, twice the proportion of
better-off households" and that "more people in the United
Kingdom die of hypothermia than in any comparable
European country" (*New Statesman & Society*, 13th August
1993). A disproportionate share of the cost of achieving
sustainability is to be carried by those least able to bear it. I
am reminded of the message sent on a postcard of an ocean
liner by Noel Coward during the Second World War. "We
may all be on a sinking ship," he wrote, "but there's no reason
why some of us shouldn't travel first class".

When the British Government issued its consultation paper
UK Strategy for Sustainable Development (HMSO 1993), Vicky
Hutchings drew attention to the all too evident fact that
sustainability is in the eye of the beholder, citing the views
expressed at the time by our endless succession of transport
ministers. One of them declared that "To halt our present
plans is to ignore the needs of industry, to ignore the fact that,
as living standards improve, there will inevitably be growth in
road traffic". And another transport minister told the House
of Lords that "Road traffic growth is largely linked to economic
growth. It would be unreasonable to set a ceiling on this". And

when, on 25th January this year the Government produced its documents with the same title, yet another transport minister was on show to declare that "There are two reasons why we build roads: to improve people's lives and to sustain the competitiveness of the British economy". You will know too, that on the previous day, the same David Pearce whose opinions I have quoted issued his book *Blueprint 3: Measuring Sustainable Development* (Earthscan, 1994) finding that Britain was using up capital faster than it was generating income from economic growth: "What tips us into the red is the failure to take account of the environment".

He is head of environmental economics at University College, and he told the press on 23rd January that his attack on Government policies arose from his "sheer frustration". He had finally "run out of patience" after five years of working with government. His own research, he said, showed that the £15 billion raised each year from road taxes is dwarfed by the £25 billion in 'social costs' of road use – noise, pollution, wear and tear on roads, congestion and accidents to pedestrians.

That minority of the population which attempts to think seriously about the debate on sustainability is confused by the clash of opinions and, understandably, reinforces its existing preferences with the new arguments floating around. Nowhere is this more evident than in the discussion of sustainable patterns of settlement. This was given a particular emphasis in a document issued by the Commission of the European Community in Brussels in 1990 called the *Green Paper on the Urban Environment* which has greatly influenced subsequent discussion. In the following year I chanced to be at a meeting of the Institute of British Geographers at which Brian Wilson, the then Chief Planning Adviser to the Department of the Environment, was asked his opinion of it. I found myself obliged to agree with his warning, when he explained that:

The European Commission strongly advocated the high density, compact city. The Green Paper puts forward the idealised view of the urban core, culturally diverse and exciting to live in. This is to ignore the fact, however, that many in Europe do not live in the urban cores of our older, finer cities. Certainly these should be maintained, even reproduced where the opportunity occurs, but the reality of much modern living cannot be ignored. Nor is it possible to envisage a return to a close relationship between place of work and residence. Job mobility is a characteristic of modern society and people increasingly change their place of work while continuing to live in the same location.

His observations could be expressed far more strongly. The inner city as a place of residence belongs to the very rich or the very poor, because of speculation in property values. Most European, or British, or American children grow up in suburbs, and the fact that by their teens they yearn to be somewhere else, does not affect the likelihood that with a rational choice among the options open to them, they will not choose to rear their own families in the high-density compact city. Only above a certain level of affluence does freedom of choice arise. It is the same with the issue of job mobility. The days when people spent a working lifetime in the same job, and consequently lived close to it, are over.

This is a matter, not just of economic trends, but of deliberate government policy. Ministers use the phrase 'flexible labour markets' to describe their policy. This is a euphemism for the absence of job security, and it explains the whittling away of legislation for Labour protection, from minimum wage agreements to conditions of employment. People desperate for a job as a source of income have no choice but to undertake long journeys to work, and very often, because of the inadequacies of public transport, to undertake them by car.

Yet, somehow, the debate on sustainable development has been whittled down to a highly academic discussion of reducing transport dependency, without reference to job security, availability of affordable housing, and adequacy of public transport. It is a debate which also ignores the fact that above a certain income level, people have freedom of choice, and below that level, people have no choice at all, while the use of the fiscal system to make citizens pay for their demands on the environment, hits them hardest.

But the issue of sustainable human settlements is precisely the area of the argument where Frederic Osborn, and his mentor Ebenezer Howard, step in. A century ago, Howard had heard, as a humble shorthand-writer, the continual debates on the horrors of the grotesquely overcrowded Victorian city, and on the disaster of rural depopulation as the rural poor fled the land that could no longer provide them a living. He produced his Garden City proposals as an alternative to endless suburbs, optimistically believing that removing the pressure of population would force down site values in the cities to allow redevelopment on a humane scale. The upper classes, of course, had a country seat to escape to from their town house, the middle classes were moving to the inner suburbs thanks to the railway network, followed by the skilled working classes, thanks to trams, the "gondolas of the people" as Richard Hoggart called them.

Ninety years ago, Howard remarked (at the London School of Economics) that "while the age we live in is the age of the great, closely compacted, overcrowded city, there are already signs, for those who can read them, of a coming change so great and so momentous that the twentieth century will be known as the period of the great exodus". This particular prophecy turned out to be true, and it is sobering to think how much greater the crisis of the cities would have been if the outward flow had not happened. For in the absence of legislation to recoup for the community the increase in site values that the presence of the urban population engendered, all through my lifetime inner city manual jobs have been killed off as firm's sites became more valuable to property speculators than the firm's output. We saw this in London in the asset-stripping 1960s and 1970s, and we saw it again in the Docklands of the 1980s.

Howard boldly embarked on his two under-funded demonstration garden cities at Letchworth and Welwyn, picking up en route as a rent collector, his ablest disciple Frederic J. Osborn. We owe the post-war New Towns programme, with both its successes and its failures, to Osborn's tireless lobbying. In the days when it was taken for granted that it was a responsibility of government to maintain full employment, the New Towns were remarkably successful in the aim of reducing the journey to work, And if by some miracle of longevity, Frederic Osborn's lifespan had been extended from 93 to something approaching 120, he would be here today, fulminating about the absurdity of making an

artificial polarity between inner city and garden city, and
pointing out that the whole garden city and New Towns
movement was intended as an alternative to endless suburbs
and what he called "the appalling cost in time and cash of long
distance commuting". and added carbon consumption on

The issues involved were discussed with great good humour
by David Lock, here in the fourth Osborn Memorial Lecture
in 1991 ('The Propaganda of the Built Environment' in *RSA
Journal*, June 1991), and I myself devoted a chapter to it in
the book I was commissioned to write about the lessons of the
New Towns. In retrospect, one of the most important things
about the post-war programme of new and expanded towns
was that it was the one item of public policy that enabled
wage-earning, rent-paying, blue-collar workers to join the
exodus that was taken absolutely for granted by the more
affluent and mobile middle classes. That route is now firmly
closed by government policy. New Towns are like anywhere
else in having their homeless young people and young families,
shut out of the housing market.

In the development boom of the late 1980s, endless
proposals for new settlements were fed into the planning
control system, none of them making more than a token
gesture to what we have now learned to call 'affordable' rented
housing, nor to the generation of new industrial jobs. In 1990
the Department of the Environment commissioned a report
on *Alternative Development Patterns: New Settlements* from
Professors Michael Breheny and David Lock. Long delayed
as politically sensitive, it was published, several ministers later,
in December 1993. It is an important document, and of
course, like everyone else, I draw from it confirmation of my
own preconceptions.

I learn that it is folly to imagine that future residential
development can or should be confined to existing cities,
towns and villages. Policies of 'town-cramming', as Osborn
argued for decades, worsen the urban environment, and run
directly contrary to hopes of 'greening the city'. Look at the
lesson of all those allotment sites and former school playing
fields, sacrificed in the development boom just to raise a bit
of income for hard-pressed local authorities. Policies of

'village-cramming' have a similar effect, as you can learn from Clive Aslett's cautionary tale of a Gloucestershire village in his book *Countryblast* (John Murray, 1991).

We do need new settlements, and the planners' dilemma is how to fit them into structure plans and local plans, as well as into the new criterion of sustainability. They are faced by consortia of developers with a battery of public relations consultants manipulating a pile of neo-ruralist imagery, as well as with the outraged nature-conservation lobby and the NIMBY (Not In My Back Yard) syndrome. So they have to calculate the advantage that can be won in the public interest through that deformation of the planning process known as 'Planning Gain'. They know all too well that their judgement will be challenged, expensively, at a Public Enquiry and a referral to the Minister. So they study the nuances of contradictory Planning Policy Guidance Notes from central government as well as the carefully laid hints contained in ministerial speeches. They are like the faithful, watching for a smoke signal to emerge from a chimney behind the facade of the Vatican.

Breheny and Lock examine nearly 200 new settlement proposals put forward since 1980, virtually all emerging from the development industry, and they conclude that the promotion of new settlements through the planning system should be encouraged, and that speculative proposals should be discouraged. This does not remove the planners' dilemma on the issue of sustainability. They know, just as you and I know, that the residents of Granary Grove and Maltings Walk will be commuters, not only to the absolute necessity of work (if they are to pay the mortgage) but to the shopping centre outside their nearest major town, and to their children's school and to the hospital serving their sick, since alleged economies of scale have determined that public facilities should serve the biggest possible catchment area. And since Breheny and Lock tell us that "work, business and education trips now account for only a third of all trips made", we can be sure that the holiday-making classes will have long-distance journeys to the nearest airport. Planning is a rather minor activity of government, and it is not reasonable to assume that, on its own, it can cope with these issues.

Another vital issue, central to Ebenezer Howard's Garden Cities proposals and the New Towns experience until central government decided to sell off New Town assets, is raised by Breheny and Lock, when they say that:

To propose that the betterment (or a part thereof) arising from the uplift in the value of land as it converts to urban use should be captured for the benefit of the community can be regarded as a political argument. This we cannot accept: the increase in value arises from the pressures of urbanisation exerted by the community, and it is wasteful and unfair that the betterment arising from the community's needs should be appropriated by the individuals or corporations who happen to own the necessary land in the place and at the time it is required.

Now my title began with the word 'self-help' and I want to conclude by inserting this concept into the discussion of sustainable settlements. Nearly twenty years ago I was asked to address the Garden Cities / New Towns Forum at Welwyn Garden City and chose as my topic 'The Do-it-yourself New Town' (reprinted in *Talking Houses*, Freedom Press, 1990). I observed that:

... a lot of people it, the town-making business: chairmen, general managers, and all their hierarchy, have had a marvellous and fulfilling time, wheeler-dealing their babies into maturity. They have been the creators, the producers. The residents, the citizens, have been the consumers, the recipients of all that planning, architecture and housing: not to mention the jobs in the missile factory. Now we are 25 years or more older, wiser and humbler. A new generation is turning upside down all those cherished shibboleths about planning, architecture and housing, not to mention the one about jobs.

I urged that we should absorb the positive lessons of the 'plotlands' of south-east England. The word is a useful bit of planners' jargon for those places where, during the agricultural depression from the turn of the century until 1939, speculators sold off plots in Essex, Kent, Sussex and the Thames Valley, to low-income Londoners to build their dream home, chicken farm, holiday shack or chalet. The existence of such places was one of the reasons for the rise of conservation bodies and comprehensive planning legislation. But when allowed to develop at their own pace such places evolved into the normal kind of suburban settlement. I claimed that:

Now we are once again in a period with a huge range of ideas in the air, especially among the young. There is the enormous interest in what has become known as alternative technology. There is, for obvious reasons, a sudden burst of interest in domestic food production, and there is an enormous new interest in alternative forms of housing, once again for obvious reasons: there are vast numbers of people whose faces or lifestyles don't fit in either the Director of Housing's office or the Building Society office ... There are large numbers of people interested in alternative ways of making a living: looking for labour-intensive low-capital industries, because capital-intensive industries have failed to provide them with an income.

So what I urged was a Do-It-Yourself New Town: an area with waivers on the planning and building legislation, where it should be possible to operate some kind of *usufruct*, some kind of leasehold with safeguards against purely cynical exploitation, which would enable people to house themselves and provide themselves with a means of livelihood, while not draining immense sums from central or local government. I make no apology for quoting from myself, partly because one of my influences on that occasion was tonight's chairman. I am referring to the article 'Non-plan: an Experiment in Freedom' by Reyner Banham, Paul Barker, Peter Hall and Cedric Price in *New Society* for 2nd March 1969. But partly, too, because years later I had the opportunity to work with Dennis Hardy on a detailed study of the plotlands of south-east England, which resulted in our book *Arcadia for All: the legacy of a makeshift landscape* (Mansell, 1984). The personal life-histories we gathered suggest that, simply because they had no option, many plotland settlers were conservers of resources to a degree beyond the dreams of the most zealous advocates of sustainability today. Take, for example, Mr Fred Nichols of Bowers Gifford, Essex. He had a poverty-stricken childhood in East London and an uncertain living as a casual dock worker. His plot of land 40 feet wide by ten feet deep, cost him £10 in 1934. First he put up a tent where his family camped at weekends. He gradually accumulated tools, timber and glass which he brought to the site strapped to his back as he cycled down from London. For water he sank a well in the garden. He called his house 'Perseverance'.

My attempt to propagate the DIY New Town idea was not

entirely fruitless. Frederic Osborn was there, and although I must have contradicted some cherished notions of his, he cited it in the final edition of his much-printed New Towns book (F.J. Osborn and Arnold Whittick, *New Towns, Their Origins, Achievements and Progress*, Leonard Hill, 1977). It gained some support within the Development Corporation at Milton Keynes. Their chairman, Lord Campbell of Eskan, was also the Town and Country Planning Association chairman and in 1988 urged the Association to promote a new, alternative community, a proposal taken up with alacrity by the Greentown Group there. It foundered on the rocks of the planning system. It was taken up again at Telford New Town leading after immense effort at Lightmoor, not to the anticipated 400 homes but to 14 (the sagas of these ventures are related in Dennis Hardy, *From New Towns to Green Politics*, Spon, 1991).

Ideas change. Two at least of those despised plotland settlements, at Dungeness and at Swansea, have actually been declared Conservation Areas by their local planning authorities. If I was optimistic in 1975 about the number of people, disowned by the employment system and the housing system, who yearned for a chance to do their own thing, and yearned too for a chance to develop their own personal and social expectations in the margins of our big-spending wasteful society, I certainly do not exaggerate their numbers today. The Town and Country Planning Association, in pursuit of its Third Garden City Proposals, convened in the 1970s a whole series of working parties, on topics from schooling to sewerage, on how to achieve a more local and sustainable mode of operation. I think it is time to dust off those reports and test them against the criteria of sustainability in 1994, and of how it can be approached without automatically penalising the poor.

One of the first essentials is that of making land available at existing use value and not at an unearned price based on its alleged value as housing land. The happy end of the Cold War, for example, has left a series of redundant military air bases, publicly owned and provided with roads and mains services. Here is a marvellous chance for a great public gesture to make

NIMBY-free land available for groups of unemployed people to build their own dream houses, with workshops and chicken-runs, kitchen gardens and tree-planting, In no time at all there would be food co-ops and community buses. Wind generators would spring up. The planners' dilemma is that of how to accommodate these dreams of self-help and sustainability while excluding those whose interest is in unsustainable profitability.

9. High Roads and Low Roads

It has been my fate to visit a great many schools of architecture in several countries, and one thing that usually happens is that my hosts, who are architects, feel obliged to apologise to the visiting examiner for the premises they occupy, on the seventh floor of the Arts Tower. which is too hot and sun-ridden in summer and too stuffy in winter, and where they cannot move a partition or shift a power point without applying for permission decided by committees at a very high level and without involving the institution in a great deal of expenditure in bringing in building contractors.

My favourite, by far, was Hull School of Architecture, housed in a solid old Victorian primary school, as it wasn't a very important department of the institution, where staff and students could do what they liked to the building, as it didn't matter. Its great glory was that its heart was the bar and canteen, a central hall, endlessly knocked about, which had become the natural meeting place of staff and students, and the place where the individual miseries that afflict some people were eased by human contact. Other people would say the same thing about the Architectural Association in London, housed in several of those infinitely adaptable buildings: English Georgian town houses.

Needless to say, when I was in Hull last year, as the process known as academic drift had made the University of Humberside out of the humbler educational institutions of

Lecture to the course on Interdisciplinary Design for the Built Environment, Magdalene College, Cambridge, 18th September 1995.

Kingston-Upon-Hull, the School of Architecture had been moved into buildings better suited to its status. I absorbed a similar lesson twelve years ago in Cambridge, Massachusetts. I remember how, together with my host, a professor of architecture at MIT, I was smoking out of the window, behind closed doors, but my lasting recollection was my guided walk-around from another friend with no architectural connections. She took me to Tent City, whose occupants were echoing a famous housing struggle in Boston by demanding that three houses in Blanche Street, illegally emptied of their occupants by the landowners MIT, should be made available to the homeless, rather than be developed as a luxury hotel and shopping complex. And she also took me to see a vast structure, called Building 20, which had been rushed up during the war and was scheduled for redevelopment by MIT, but which was remembered as the place where endless innovations in communications science and a whole range of inventions were born. It struck me at the time as an illustration of the general rule that the moment any institution invests in a new purpose-built headquarters, its useful days are over.

Because, from my standpoint, I take this for granted, I had forgotten this visit, but it has been brought back to me by a new book, Stewart Brand's *How Buildings Learn: What Happens After They're Built* (Penguin/ Viking, 1994). He classifies buildings as High Road, Low Road and No Road, and I find this a useful vocabulary for classifying my hopes and fears about the urban environment.

The two kind of buildings that, as he puts it, "easily become loved" are on the High Road and the Low Road equally. On the High Road they are "durable, independent buildings that steadily accumulate experience and become in time wiser and more respected than their inhabitants". Maybe these ancient Cambridge colleges are among these, endlessly adapted to new needs over generations. Brand is withering at the expense of that dreadful historicism among conservationists that demands that the accumulated additions, alterations and adaptations or extensions of centuries should be swept away to expose some imagined architectural integrity of the 'original' design, whether of the eighteenth century or the twentieth. Every farmhouse, cottage or city street represents the accretions of centuries, and every semi-detached suburban house, so despised by the architectural opinion-formers of the 1920s and 1930s, has become an expensive and desirable property by the 1990s, not only by generations of use, but because the trees and bushes have matured along with the buildings.

Along the Low Road are endless utilitarian structures, never blessed by architects: shop-fronts, sheds and garages, factory buildings, pump-houses and school-rooms, which, as Brand puts it, are swiftly responsive to their occupants, and are "unrespectable, mercurial, street-smart". To my delight, Building 20 in Vassar Street, Cambridge, Massachusetts, was still there when he wrote. I learn that it was designed in an afternoon in 1943 by Don Whiston, three-storeyed and timber-framed because the war made steel unavailable, and was occupied six months later by radar researchers. The building was given a temporary licence by the city council because it contravened the fire regulations, though Broad reports that just because it wasn't designed for a specific, finely-worked-out purpose, it is one of the strongest buildings on campus, capable of bearing 150 pounds per square foot of floor.

And although it was about to be demolished when I was there in the property boom of the late 1980s, I learn that it is still functioning. Brand notes that "The science of linguistics was largely started there, and forty years later in 1993 one of its pioneers, Noam Chomsky, was still rooted there".

Stewart Brand tries not to romanticise Building 20. He notes that, just like a lot of grander structures it is "too hot in the summer, too cold in the winter, spartan in its amenities, often dirty, and implacably ugly". It is festooned internally by easy-to-change pipes, tubes and wiring, and on the outside by overnight "sprouted outgrowths". Brand asked the retired president of MIT how Building 20 had lasted so long. There were three answers. The first was that "At 300 dollars a square foot, it would take 75 million dollars to replace". The second was that "It's a very matter-of-fact building. It puts on the personality of the people in it". His final answer was that when he was made president of the university, he kept a hideaway office there, because that was where "nobody complained when you nailed something to a door".

The character that he ascribes to that building apply to whole streets that you and I will have observed in towns both in Britain and abroad. But before leaving *How Buildings Learn*, I have to mention his other category: No Road Buildings. These are prestige buildings designed by architects to impress other architects through photographs in magazines, made before they were occupied. He is frank about I.M. Pei's Wiesner Building at MIT, which "hogs space, isolates and overwhelms people, and provides no amenities", or about Jim Stirling's history-faculty building at Cambridge, England, which "leaked badly, kept dropping terracotta tiles on the students, and faced the wrong way, so the sun cooked its contents – people and books". If he was really malicious he could list a lot of other buildings by these and other architects admired by the people we tolerate as opinion-formers in the architectural world.

When we shift to a wider perspective than the individual building to the street it has taken over, everyone's experience is that the important and useful resources we rely on are round the corner from the high street or main street which is full of multiple retailers, banks and building societies, and in the places where site values are low enough to support a multiplicity of specialist services which could not yield the site rents of new buildings in rebuilt streets. These Really Useful Streets certainly contain some High Road buildings. There is for example the Public Library, probably donated to the town by Andrew Carnegie at the turn of the century, which has adapted itself to the new demands of the end of the century. Recent research by the body called Comedia, shows that, like the public park, the public library is the most heavily used of all resources available to all, young and old, rich and poor, and has adapted itself to changing needs. There are other High Road structures, like churches, which today could be anything from local history museums to bingo halls. Lovers of the inner East End of London will point to a building, just outside the City to avoid its persecution of non-conformity, which has been in succession, a Huguenot chapel, a non-conformist meeting house, a synagogue, and now a mosque.

The constraints of the size of sites, inhibiting High Road buildings, encouraged the survival of the Low Road. In British towns, sites in the medieval central core had an ancient 'burgage' width of up to 10 metres, which tended to dictate the scale of redevelopment until the days of compulsory purchase orders. In American cities, Brand cites the view of an urban designer Anne Vernez Moudon who noted how:

Small lots will support resilience because they allow many people to attend directly to their needs by designing, building, and maintaining their own environment. By ensuring that property remains in many hands, small lots bring important results: many people make many different decisions, thereby ensuring variety in the resulting environment. And many property owners slow down the rate of change by making large-scale real estate transactions difficult.

She is raising an everyday experience for all of us. When I was a city dweller I only once lived within walking distance of my work. We lived in a quiet street of 1890s houses, just off a main road which was, however, a Low Road in Stewart Brand's terms. In my quarter-hour walk to work I passed, not only a series of public services like the library, the ambulance and fire station, even the police station, but the whole range of the usual small shops, pubs and sellers of spare parts, and also the repairer of washing machines and household appliances (televisions were dealt with by one of the men from the ambulance station) and the wood shop which sold cut-to-size bits of hardboard, blackboard or formica and half a dozen screws of any variety you needed.

Whenever I go back there to see old friends I notice the disappearance of more and more of those services which I actually valued. I can't blame this on large-scale redevelopment. It is, far more, due to the determination of landlords to squeeze the last ounce of rent from properties they bought up in the boom years, and to the effect of the Uniform Business Rate. In plenty of other places where wholesale redevelopment was engineered into being by ambitious local authorities, like, say, Newcastle-upon-Tyne, the first thing that strikes the enquiring wanderer like me is that individual buildings have been designed in isolation. I don't worry about that, but what I always notice is that they are separated, like detached houses in an estate agent's window, with open space and a wall or railing between them. Party walls, which used to be hidden behind a continuous street elevation, are now a visible manifestation of discontinuity. When you ask the architects how this came about, they blame the requirements of the local authority planners for car parking at the rear or of the fire officer for access all around.

Now what is destroyed is that very, elusive quality that we call urbanity. In visual terms this simply refers to the effect of the continuous elevation which can be found in tiny villages as much as in large towns. My own local village, Kersey in Suffolk, was one of Raymond Unwin's exemplars in his book *Town Planning in Practice* and is much visited by coach-loads of people who walk up and down, feed the ducks, and annoy the posh residents by peering through their windows. They do so because there's nowhere to go inside now the shop has closed, except the two pubs, the church, and the excellent pottery whose wares are made on the spot. If I were young and entrepreneurial I would open a teashop and bookshop selling anarchist literature and town-planning tracts. Such a planning application, however, would have been fought tooth and nail, by the residents, as was a recent attempt by two parish councillors to introduce a housing association proposal for 'affordable' housing.

I was recently in a little Devon town, Buckfastleigh, where, once again, there was this continuous street facade on a humbler and more useful scale. It was punctuated by archways and alley-ways leading to backland development of cheap cottages, workshops, traders and car repairers, with low rents for sub-standard property in the Low Road scene of endless adaptability. The High Road has been the scene of endless loss of the amenities that matter to people like us. One of the books I want to recommend to you is Ken Worpole's *Towns for People: transforming urban life* (Open University Press, 1992). He describes how the shift of the 'centre' in several towns to new shopping precincts has left High Road buildings like the theatre, main library and municipal buildings, "relatively isolated". And he points out that the success of the multiple retailers has been at the expense not only of the environment, but of the local economy:

Only the multiples have been able to afford the rent in the new malls and high street locations and local firms have been driven out of business. Between 1960 and 1989 the multiples increased their share of the retailing sales from 33% to 80%, giving them the giant's share of the market and of the town centre. It was rare to find in or near town-centre sites, specialist shops such as picture framers, craft and artists' materials, health-food shops, antiques, wine-making and home brewing, cycle shops, hobby shops, radio repairers second-hand bookshops, and many of the other shops that reflect an active participation in leisure. In Truro most of the local traders who accounted for nearly 80% of shops and stalls, have vanished from the city centre. In Southend people complained that it was no longer possible to buy a pint of milk in the High Street; in Basingstoke people said that it was difficult to buy a tin of paint. The displacement of other activities can be seen most graphically in the case of Bath where, in 1988, crane manufacturers Stothert & Pitt, one of the West Country's oldest firms, learned that it was to be broken up and sold by its new owners to release its town-centre site for redevelopment; high land values had made the site much more valuable for shops, offices and leisure facilities than for manufacturing.

There is a similar message in a book of my own, *Welcome, Thinner City* (1989), which I only mention as it is available at an absurdly low price, in which I have a chapter called 'Death of the Fine-Grain City'. There I quote the opinions of the Association for Urban Quality in Birmingham, commenting on yet another proposal to re-develop, wholesale, the Bull Ring Centre in that city:

Essentially it is *too big*. In the traditional city, street blocks reduced in size the nearer they are to the centre. There are good reasons for this. In a city centre the mixture of uses and buildings gets more complex, and they are all competing for street frontage. The *smaller* the blocks are, the more street frontage there is. This relationship produces a lively city Centre – busy streets, varied activity, varied buildings.

Now suppose that, armed with this kind of observation about the High Road and the Low Road, I was asked to make recommendations about some hypothetical proposal to shift some teaching organisation from some town, where its site had become more valuable than some administrator's sense of the value of the activity itself, onto a site on the fringe of town. What would I recommend? You will have heard enough to know that I would totally discount the concept of the architect as master designer. Cambridge has had plenty of that already. I would concentrate on the role of the architect as wheeler-dealer, fixer and adapter, which ought to have been a familiar role from John Nash onwards, and I would look for some perimeter site where public money had been expended in the past to provide an industrial estate where starter factories had been erected, and had never actually started. Nothing new about this: I know of places where, in desperation, the public authority landlord has let in snooker clubs or bingo halls. These would become the equivalent of Building 20 in Cambridge, Massachusetts. There is nothing new about this kind of educational approach. It is a quarter of a century since the architects Robert Maguire and Keith Murray found that the best way of building their primary school at Bow Common in East London was to use a standard agriculture shed imaginatively (fully evaluated in *British School Build*, edited by Colin Ward, Architectural Press, 1976).

Let's assume that part of the task of the designer is to use any space for any purpose and that the money should be spent on ingenuity rather than on architectural egos. The more challenging task is in all those ancillaries that make any place a habitat. I'm sure that the first of these is the tea-room-cafeteria-restaurant-bar, open all hours. And the next is every retail outlet that can be encouraged. These will need a lot of coaxing. In the New Town programme, believing in the neighbourhood shop, the New Town Corporations gave uneconomic rents to uneconomic shop-keepers. When market ideology took over, the shops just closed. Money spent on making services work is more important than money spent on building. And (who knows?) if students could be encouraged to live on site, and to spend evenings manning those services, it might be possible to convert some of those unleased factories into low-rent housing. The harbour district of Amsterdam is full of creative squatter adaptations of dead warehouses.

It might be possible to fill the gaps between sites with Walter Segal-type self-built student accommodation, equipping them

with valuable know-how in timber-framed construction, de-
mystifying the building business, but also providing valuable
experience in coping with all the multitudinous sources of
authority that stand in the way of anyone doing anything in
this country.

What a triumph it would be, to create a living example of a
convivial urban centre by exploiting the creativity of people,
rather than by adding to the profits of the major building
contractors! When the then current dictator of Brazil instituted
the new capital city of High Road buildings, Brasilia, visiting
diplomats, salesmen and educators used to be told that to have
the authentic flavour of Brazilian food, music or hospitality,
they should go to the *cidades libres* outside the city where the
building tradesmen who built it lived. If we were bold enough
to leave the High Road property speculators to survive in the
mess they have made, we might make new Low Roads out on
the fringe.

10. The anarchist house

I have to begin with problems of definition. We have no problem with the word *house*. We have few problems with the associated word *home* which adds an emotional significance to the first word. We have a *house* and we make it into a *home*.

My difficulties arise with the word *anarchist*. The hero of Vladimir Nabokov's novel *Pnin* is asked "Are you an anarchist?" And, very unwisely, he replies with a question for his interrogator: "First, what do we understand under *anarchism*? Anarchism practical, metaphysical, theoretical, mystical, abstractional, individual, social?" It did him no good. He spent two weeks on Ellis Island, before he was allowed to enter the USA.

I have a similar problem. I want to be open to every possible definition of anarchism, but I have to exclude plenty of interpretations simply to say something useful.

The first item of ballast that I have to throw overboard is the idea that there is an anarchist aesthetic, in opposition to bourgeois aesthetics. For a century in all the arts, visual, literary or aural, it has been assumed that the task of revolutionary artists is to stupefy the bourgeoisie. Having been stupefied for many decades, during which real life has been far more shocking than the arts, it is still the bourgeoisie who are the only effective customers for all that revolutionary art. Apart, that is, from the State.

In the visual arts, for example, the most obvious allies for the anarchists were the Surrealists, but with notable exceptions, the closest political links *they* sought were with the Communist Party. In Britain, the most celebrated artist with links to the anarchist movement was an academic painter of

Lecture at the conference on Libertarian Culture, Grenoble, March 1996

bohemian habits, whose reputation probably did not travel.
This was Augustus John (1878-1961) who is remembered,
not as an anarchist, but as the last of the great classical
draughtsmen. And the most famous of all anarchist artists,
Camille Pissarro (1831-1903), closely linked with the anarchist
movement of his day, steadfastly declined to specify the
content of an anarchist aesthetic. His letters ignore syntax and
grammar and are absorbing human documents. The closest
he gets to defining an anarchist aesthetic is in Volume III of
his collected correspondence, where he says:

Y a-t-il un art anarchiste? quoi décidément ils ne comprennent pas. Tous
les arts sont anarchistes quand c'est beau et bien![1]

When we consider the art of architecture, the assumption that
there is a specifically anarchist aesthetic becomes even more
questionable. Many of us will remember a side-show in fair-
grounds or amusement parks called 'The Crazy House'. We
paid our pennies to experience a simulated house where the
floors and ceilings were not parallel and where the walls, doors
and windows were not rectilinear.

Much more recently, this kind of Crazy House architecture
has been built seriously in real life. For example, at Montréal,
Canada, for the World's Fair in the 1970s, Moshe Safdie
designed the Habitat apartments where each flat is dropped
apparently at random in an accidental-looking pile of containers.
In practise, of course, every aspect of this chance arrangement
was carefully calculated by structural engineers. Similarly in
the Oude Haven (Old Harbour) area of Rotterdam you can
visit a cloister of tilted houses designed by the architect Piet
Blom, which are a solid reminder of the Crazy House structure
in the Fun Fair.

If you imagine yourself as a building worker, living in a
cramped apartment in a block of flats, and employed on the
building of one of those architectural fantasies, you will readily
agree that fantasy architecture is not anarchist architecture. It
provides no liberation for the people involved in building it,
and the joke of disobeying aesthetic assumptions probably gets
stale rapidly for the people who live in it. The issue is not a
matter of design, but is a question of *control*, a far more

important aspect of the anarchist spectrum.

For me, the first principle of housing in any society, quite apart from the ideal for an anarchist society, is dweller control. We are fortunate that this principle has been very carefully enunciated by an anarchist architect, John Turner. He spent many years in the 1950s and 1960s assisting self-builders in squatter settlements in Latin America. He then moved to the United States and learned that the ideas he had formulated in the poor world were true of the richest nation in the world. And when he finally returned to Britain he found that the housing situation in his own country also fitted his formulation.[2] Turner's key insight is this:

When dwellers control the major decisions and are free to make their own contribution to the design, construction or management of their housing, both the process, and the environment produced, stimulate individual and social well-being. When people have no control over, nor responsibility for, key decisions in the housing process, on the other hand, dwelling environments may instead become a barrier to personal fulfilment and a burden on the economy.[3]

This is a carefully-worded statement that says no more and no less than it means. Notice that Turner refers to "design, construction or management". He is not implying that we should all become *bricoleurs* or do-it-yourself house-builders, although of course, in practice, this is what people often have to be. He is stating as a principle that *they* should be in control.

I would like you to notice particularly his last sentence about dwelling environments which become "a barrier to personal fulfilment and a burden on the economy". Is this not the experience of huge, expensive housing projects undertaken by central and local governments, both in the United States and all around Western Europe? The only solution to the problems of these projects is to develop systems of dweller control through the various forms of housing co-operatives. Sometimes, in those vast housing projects on the outskirts of European and American cities as a legacy of bureaucratic managerial socialism, tenant control is adopted as a last desperate measure in the face of dereliction and decay. There is a well-known architect, Lucien Kroll of the *Atelier d'Urbanisme et d'Architecture* at Bruxelles. He is often asked to advise on the exercise of making habitable big, neglected municipal housing projects in France, Germany and the Netherlands.

The results are often described as anarchist architecture. Lucien Kroll insists, on the other hand, that it is dweller-controlled architecture. He told me that the *first* task, not the last, is to present residents with a budget for *them* to decide the priorities in expenditure. Do they want money spent first on improving the insulation in wells, or on making the building too publicly visible to be infiltrated by drug traffickers?

One general priority is to reduce the scale of buildings by removing a few storeys (*étages*) from the top and to have more building at ground level in the spaces between blocks. Another is the issue of 'traffic calming'. Would it be sensible to use the concrete rubble from the reduction of height of blocks to build a little hill on a road roundabout, planted with bushes and trees as an inescapable vehicle-hazard that kept traffic out? How about digging up the municipal grass to make playgrounds and allotments (*jardins potager*), and building an accretion of workshops and cafes as lean-to (*appentis*) extensions around the base of the towers? The results may not be anarchist architecture, but they are certainly *post-authoritarian* architecture.

Although Britain is seen as the country of origin of the co-operative movement, housing co-operatives are much more recent there than in many other countries. In the 1970s there were only two or three. Today there are about a thousand. This is a pathetically small number, and this indicates how far we are from separating control from ownership, since in Britain the preferred mode of tenure is owner-occupation (66%). But its composition is interesting. Some started through the legitimisation of squatter occupation of empty buildings. Some originated in 'short-life housing' (buildings awaiting demolition). Under conditions of dweller-control this short-life housing has had a very long life, simply because of the incentives the occupants have to improve it. Some, in Liverpool and London, are newly-built housing, where the architect worked to the instructions of poor people who, for the first time in their lives were able to employ expertise.[4]

But the most interesting are in the dweller-built sector. All through history, throughout the world, poor people have constructed their own homes, which were improved and expanded over decades and centuries, as families turned their labour into capital. The evidence can be seen in traditional peasant farmhouses in most parts of Europe. In the twentieth century this simple and natural way of building has become increasingly difficult for a variety of reasons.

The first is the key issue of access to land. In Britain the process known as 'Enclosure' ensured that land which was once described as common or 'waste', now has a legal owner. The second is in the nature of building materials. Once the self-builder would automatically use stone, clay, timber and straw from the locality, so that the house, as an English poet said, would "rise like a lark from the furrows". Twentieth century houses are constructed from materials which, whether they are natural or synthetic, have to be bought in the market. The third reason is of course, that we have surrounded the process of building with a pile of legislation and regulations which is incomprehensible to the citizen without professional help.

One English architect (of German origin) who surmounted these obstacles was Walter Segal (1907-1985). He, incidentally, was reared in an anarchist commune in Ticino, Switzerland.[5] Late in life he developed a method of lightweight timber-framed construction, using standard building components in standard sizes, and eliminating the 'wet' trades of concreting, brick-laying and plastering. It was eminently suited to the amateur builder. He was yearning for it to be made available to people in need of housing, and one London municipality decided to provide an opportunity, on plots of land too small or too sloping to be used by the council itself.[6]

The result was a triumph of dweller satisfaction. Members of the group described the experience as the event which changed their lives and felt that they were in control. And it was the happiest event in the life of their veteran architect. Segal recalled that:

Help was to be provided mutually and voluntarily – there were no particular constraints on that, which did mean that the good will of people could find its way through. The less you tried to control them the more you forced the

element of good will – this was astonishingly clear. Children were of course
expected and allowed to play on the site. And the older ones also helped if
they wished to help. That way one avoided all forms of friction. Each family
were to build at their own speed and within their own capacity. We had
(quite a number of young people, but some who were sixty and over, who
also managed to build their own houses ... They were told that I would not
interfere with their internal arrangements. I let them make their own
decisions; therefore we had no difficulties.[7]

He noted with pleasure, rather than with irritation, the
"countless small variations and innovations and additions"
that the self-builders made. His conclusion was that "It is
astonishing that there is among the people that live in this
country such a wealth of talent." Since this architect's death,
the Walter Segal Self-Build Trust has successfully promoted
his approach among a whole series of disadvantaged groups
in the bleak political climate of the 1990s.[8] It always takes far
longer to overcome the obstacles of finance and permissions
and the planning and building legislation, than it does for the
self-builders to construct and occupy their homes.

I have described the anarchist house in terms of real
experiences among ordinary citizens in the world of today. But
in view of the varieties of definitions of the word anarchism, I
should explore a few other aspects. Some of us try very hard
to bridge the gap between real life and anarchist theory over
day-to-day issues like housing. Among the well-known theorists,
Kropotkin is full of interest. His chapter on 'Dwellings' in his
book on *The Conquest of Bread* (in French 1892, in English
1906) was, essentially, his manual on what should happen in
a revolutionary society: an equitable share-out of existing
housing according to needs.

Most of us do not live in revolutionary situations but still
need to house our families and get by in whatever kind of
society we chance to inhabit. Here, I think, another classical
anarchist is a better guide. This was, of course, Pierre-Joseph
Proudhon, who in a famous, but unreadable, book *What is
Property?* (1840), coined the slogan that "Property is Theft".
I'm like anyone else. I rejoiced on that day in September 1969,
when the squatters at a former royal residence at 144 Piccadilly
in London suspended a banner with Proudhon's slogan in
metre-high letters.

But one of the ironies noted by Proudhon's critics was the fact that he also coined the slogan "Property is Freedom". It ought not to be necessary to explain that the first Slogan was directed at the absentee landowner, defined by George Woodcock as "the man who uses it to exploit the labour of others without any effort on his own part, property distinguished by interest and rent, by the impositions of the non-producer on the producer". The other kind of property, he explained, was that of the owner-occupier or peasant cultivator, and 'possession', or the right to control the dwelling and the land and tools needed to live was seen by Proudhon as "the corner stone of liberty", while "his main criticism of the Communists was that they wished to destroy it".[9]

The seventy-year history of the Union of Socialist Soviet Republics and the shorter life of the regimes it enforced upon eastern Europe provide a basis for examining Kropotkin's and Proudhon's opinions in the light of experience. There was a share-out of existing housing according to need. Most observers recorded that the needs of the Party hierarchy were more urgent than those of ordinary citizens, as of course was their need for a *dacha* in the country. Stalin's enforced collectivisation of agriculture literally liquidated the peasantry, resulting in millions of deaths and in famine. Meanwhile in the cities housing policy was an extreme version of the planners' infatuation with tower blocks that we also experienced in the West.

Slowly and subversively, Proudhonian popular attitudes began to reassert themselves. As Proudhon would have prophesied, the peasants' personal plots around their houses were the salvation of the ordinary Russian's food supply many Years before *perestroika*:

In 1963, private plots covered about 44,000 square kilometres or some 4% of all the arable land of the collective farms. From this 'private' land, however, comes about half of all the vegetables produced in the USSR, while 40% of the cows and 30% of the pigs in the country are on them.[10]

Similarly, in the 1970s the economist Hugh Stretton was reporting that: "Pathetically, Russian town dwellers go out and comb the countryside for patches of neglected land they can plant, visit, enjoy, 'make their own', however tenuously".[11] Their Marxist rulers, of course, had their *dachas*, but throughout Czechoslovakia, Hungary, Rumania and Yugoslavia, city dwellers were building their real life around what were called 'wild settlements' outside the city. Thus in 1979, a geographer was explaining that:

The existence of peasant-owned land on the fringes of cities offers opportunities for piecemeal evolution – indeed 'overnight mushrooming' of 'wild settlements' as in Nowy Dwòr and elsewhere outside Warsaw or in Kozarski Bok and Trnje on the margins of Zagreb. Such communities are not encouraged, yet they are tolerated and even provided with utilities and welfare since they relieve some of the pressures on city housing and budgets.[12]

Observations like these, from the days when it was still assumed that the Communist regimes of Eastern Europe were expected to have a future, are a reminder to revolutionaries of every kind, of the importance of Proudhon's careful distinction between property as exploitation and property as possession.

Communism, enforced by terror, has brought an inevitable individualist reaction, and has tarnished every variety of socialist aspiration. But there has always been a quieter, gentler, libertarian advocacy of communal living. Together with other ideologists, both secular and religious, many anarchists have been critical of the nuclear family and of the one-family dwelling that is the universal provision for it. Like other critics, they have seen the individual house as a prison for its inhabitants and have sought a wider social unit. Thus Kropotkin declared:

Today we live too isolated. Private property has led us to an egotistic individualism in all our mutual relations. We know one another only slightly; our points of contact are too rare. But we have seen in history examples of a communal life which is more intimately bound together – the 'composite family' in China, the agrarian communes, for example. There people really know one another. By force of circumstances they must aid one another materially and morally.

Family life, based on the original community, has disappeared. A new family, based on community of aspirations, will take its place. In this family people will be obliged to know one another for moral support on every occasion ...[13]

Kropotkin, like Tolstoy, was the inspiration for a long series of communal ventures aiming to combine living with intensive horticulture, and their mostly short life-spans have been intensely studied in retrospect.[14] They offer us little illumination of the nature of the anarchist house, since their initiators were poor and had to make use of whatever buildings were available. But one of these failed ventures in Britain did evoke a very significant comment from Kropotkin. This was the Clousdon Hill Free Communist and Co-operative Colony, established on a twenty-acre (8 hectare) farm near Newcastle-upon-Tyne in 1895. Its founders wrote to him for advice, and the advice he gave was interesting. He warned the colonists to avoid isolation from the surrounding community, he urged that "barrack-like living conditions should be avoided in favour of combined efforts by independent families" and he wrote very sensibly about the situation of women. It was important, he wrote, to:

... do all possible for reducing household work to the lowest minimum ... In most communities this point was awfully neglected. The women and the girls remained in the new society as they were in the old – slaves of the community. Arrangements to reduce as much as possible the incredible amount of work which women uselessly spend in the rearing-up of children, as well as in the household work, are, in my opinion, as essential to the success of the community as the proper arrangements of the fields, the greenhouses, and the agricultural machinery. Even more. But while every community dreams of having the most perfect agricultural or industrial machinery, it seldom pays attention to the squandering of the forces of the house slave, the women.[15]

To my mind, this is one of Kropotkin's least-known, but most significant statements of an anarchist approach. And it has enormous relevance to any attempt to define the anarchist house. Consider classical house plans: Palladian villas, Italian *palazzi*, the English Georgian town house. They, unlike much modern architecture, were and are infinitely adaptable to innumerable uses, because they did not depend upon the endless variety of technical services – water, gas, electricity, heating systems and telecommunications – that we take for granted today. (As Le Corbusier remarked, "Heureux pour Ledoux: pas des tubes"). Instead, all these facilities were provided by human means: slaves, servants, housemaids, washer-women, messenger boys. You have only to watch *The

Marriage of Figaro to be reminded of the way in which servants were part of the architecture: the mortar that really held it together.

As personal service declined, the designers of buildings continued to give priority to what were know as 'reception rooms' and the significantly named 'master bedroom' but squeezed key service areas – the kitchen, the bathroom, the laundry room – into smaller and smaller areas. The point is well made by the American experimenter Stewart Brand. Readers may remember him as the instigator in the 1960s and 1970s of *The Whole Earth Catalog* and its imitators in many countries. He has recently re-emerged as the author of a book *How Buildings Learn: What happens after they're built,* which in many ways can be seen as a manual on the anarchist house. Here he embraces the architectural philosophy of "Long life, loose fit, low energy", demanding that every building should, from the day it is begun, have the capacity to be endlessly adapted to meet the needs of its users. Many years ago the anarchist architect Giancarlo De Carlo declared that building users have to *attack* the building to make it their own, and the phrase that Brand adopts to define his kind of anarchy is "wholesome chaos".

In an important observation on the way in which this attitude changes our approach to houses, Brand explains that:

One way to institutionalise wholesome chaos is to disperse significant design power to the individual users of a building while they're using the place. Notice the difference between kitchens designed to be used by powerless servants – they are usually dark, cramped pits – and kitchens used by the heads of a family – bright, spacious, centrally located, crammed with conveniences. A building 'learns' much faster than whole organisations. This suggests a 'bottom-up' rather than 'top-down' approach in the building's human hierarchy ... What would a building look like and act like if it was designed for easy servicing by the users themselves? Once people are comfortable doing their own maintenance and repair, re-shaping comes naturally because they have a hands-on relationship with their space, and they know how to improve it ...[16]

There are several reasons for anticipating that, while anarchist houses are marginal in the housing economy of the rich world in the twentieth century, they will become more significant in the twenty-first century. I have several reasons for this forecast. The first is the expensive failure of official housing policy in the Western countries. It was constructed around a political notion of nuclear family households. But in Britain, the United States and France, most households today do not fit the statistical norm. The system is not designed for their needs. Alternative communal households are bound to develop.

The second reason is the lesson of the poor world and the poor segments of the rich world. The unofficial population of the poor world cities is larger that that of the official city. Whenever poor people can gain access to land and materials, they build dweller-controlled housing which grows and adapts according to need and opportunity.[17]

The third reason is the impact of feminism upon housing design. As Kropotkin indicated, half the population has always been excluded from housing decisions, but as Dolores Heyden insists, there has always been an alternative approach, hidden from history.[18]

My final reason is the impact of the Green movement and of considerations of ecological sustainability. Today, every individual family house has a huge investment in energy-wasting services and equipment with an in-built short life. Rational use of power demands durable, energy-saving, and shared equipment.[19]

The technical criterion for the anarchist house is "Long life, loose fit, low energy", but the political demand is the principle of Dweller Control.

1. Janine Bailly-Herzberg (editor), *Correspondance de Camille Pissarro*, 5 volumes, (Paris: Presses Universitaires de France, et Pontoioe: Editions du Valhermeil, 1980-91).

2. Colin Ward, 'Preface' to John F.C. Turner, *Housing by People: Towards Autonomy in Building Environments* (London: Marion Boyars, 1976).

3. John Turner in John F.C. Turner and Robert Fichter (editors), *Freedom to Build: Dweller Control of the Housing Process* (New York: Macmillan, 1972).

4. Colin Ward, *Welcome, Thinner City* (London: Bedford Square Press, 1989).

5. John McKean, *Learning from Segal* (Basle: Birkhäuser Verlag, 1989).

6. Jon Broome and Brian Richardson, *The Self-Build Book* (Devon: Green Books, 1991).

7. Colin Ward, *Talking Houses* (London: Freedom Press, 1990).

8. Walter Segal Self Build Trust, 57 Chalton Street, London NW1 1HU.

9. George Woodcock, *Pierre-Joseph Proudhon, a Biography* (London: Routledge & Kegan Paul, 1956).

10. J.P. Cole, *A Geography of the USSR* (Harmondsworth: Penguin Books, 1967).

11. Hugh Stretton, *Capitalism, Socialism and the Environment* (Cambridge University Press, 1976).

12. Ian Hamilton, 'Spatial Structure in East European Cities' in F.E. French and I. Hamilton (editors) *The Socialist City* (Chichester: John Wiley, 1979).

13. Peter Kropotkin, *Prisons and their Moral Influence on Prisoners* (1877), reprinted in Baldwin (editor) *Kropotkin's Revolutionary Pamphlets* (New York: Vanguard Press, 1927; Dover Press, 1971).

14. For the British experience, see Dennis Hardy, *Alternative Communities in Nineteenth Century England* (London: Longman, 1979).

15. Peter Kropotkin, letter published, with his permission, in *Newcastle Daily Chronicle* 20th February 1895, quoted in Colin Ward's 'Colonising the Land: Utopian Ventures' in *The Raven* anarchist quarterly, No 17, (Vol 5 No 1) January-March 1992.

16. Stewart Brand, *How Buildings Learn* (New York and London: Penguin/Viking, 1994).

17. See, for example, the books by John Turner, listed above. In a British context see Dennis Hardy and Colin Ward, *Arcadia for All: The Legacy of a Makeshift Landscape* (London: Mansell, 1984).

18. Dolores Hayden, *The Grand Domestic Revolution: a History of Feminist Designs for American Homes, Neighborhoods and Cities* (Cambridge, Massachusetts: MIT Press, 1981).

19. Every European language has its own literature on this theme.

Press comments on

COLIN WARD'S

TALKING HOUSES

"Many will welcome this latest addition to the prolific Ward literature on housing. As the author himself candidly says, these ten lectures merely reiterate the – to him – simple truths he has been proclaiming for the last 45 years. He confesses that he has nothing new to say and it puzzles him that he is in perpetual demand as a pundit. He can only explain it by people wanting hands-on contact with the human propagators of ideas. Always in the vanguard of fresh examples, he does, indeed, continue to have a unique role to play."
— **Alison Ravetz in *The Architects' Journal***

"Ward believes that when people cooperate on a small scale and choose, manage and even build for themselves, they get better housing than when governments make choices for them. Decades of official directives and central control have kept us from a great state secret: human beings are, unless culturally disabled, well qualified to meet their essential needs – food, shelter and conviviality."
— **Peter Campbell in *New Statesman and Society***

"The relevance of the anarchist analysis ought to be self-evident ... This book is a valuable source of practical examples of user control and provides glimpses of a well constructed ideological framework to set them in ... conveyed with absolute clarity."
— **Benjamin Derbyshire in *RIBA Journal***

"Labour's policy on housing has not yet gone on the offensive in reappropriating the language and spirit of self-help and local control so that people no longer fear that regulation is its knee-jerk solution to all problems. The party could usefully borrow from Ward's exhilarating polemic in support of changing the role of the administration from providers to enablers, of the citizens from recipients to participants."
— **Shaun Spiers in *Tribune***

FREEDOM PRESS   142 pages   ISBN 0 900384 55 7   £5.00